KEY WEST Today

The Very Best
153 Things
YOU MUST DO
2017/2018

by
Bucky Montgomery

© 2017

Montgomery Publishing, PO Box 375, Key West, FL 33041
buckymontgomery@gmail.com

Dedicated to two Key West 'idea' guys --
David Sloan and Christopher Shultz
for writing the book I should have --
'Quit Your Job and Move to Key West',
still the best Key West book out there.
Because I can relate. I've done it, twice.

Now, get to checkin' boxes.

Hi.

Key West, Florida. **A magical place**. A cross between the Island of Misfit Toys and Andy Griffith's Mayberry. This unique and quirky little tropical island requires no passport for American citizens. Once home to Indians, pirates, Spanish conquistadors and mosquitoes, now it is home to the eccentric, the rich and the poor, the famous and infamous, the partiers, the artists and musicians, the tourists here for a festival, and the locals, who have, for whatever reason, scratched a life for themselves here in this quaint village. Key West -- average summer temperatures 85 degrees, average winter temperatures 75 degrees. Home to wild roosters and chickens, sunbathing iguanas, six-toed cats, and year 'round bikinis. Where the closest major city is Havana, Cuba, 90 miles to the south, followed close behind by Miami, 150 miles waaay up north. Access to year 'round water sports, festivals, the arts, and North America's only living coral barrier reef. So much to do, so much to see, so much to experience. Historic and friendly, diverse and laid back.

First, 153 things doesn't come close to covering it, and is by no means comprehensive. There could be a 153 KW restaurants book, or 153 art galleries, 153 Fantasy Fest events, or 153 birds to watch for. **It's not comprehensive, but it's a good start**.

Next, **it's all subject to change**. Things come and go all the time down here: Duck Tours, Fast Buck Freddies, Bobdive, ocean jet packs, Pelican Poop, Ben Franklin...all gone. So, I'll update with each new edition. This one, as far as I know, is up to date.

It's not a countdown necessarily. The numerical significance of each event, activity, and restaurant is not in any particular order, until I got to the end. The last fifteen or so are some of the most significant.

I'm no expert. I've lived here off and on for twenty years. Once anyone has lived in Key West for two months, they consider themselves honorary tour guides. That's me. Have you done everything listed in this book? I've provided boxes for you to check off. **Let's see how well you've experienced Key West.** -- Bucky

Table of Contents (by category)

Table of Contents (by category)

Table of Contents (by category)

Mile Marker Zero

Depending on your viewpoint (or which side of the street you're on) it all starts and/or stops right here. US 1 travels along the east coast for 2,369 miles, beginning (or ending) at 490 Whitehead St., with its other end at Fort Kent, Maine, right on the Canadian border, making it the longest north-south road in the United States. One of the most popular places to have your picture taken on the island.

Type: Photo Op
Cost: Free
When: Anytime

Located at the corner of Whitehead and Fleming Streets

Escape the hustle and bustle and stroll through a magical and breathtaking climate-controlled glass-enclosed butterfly habitat filled with hundreds of the most beautiful winged creatures found in nature. Mingle with more than fifty butterfly species from around the world, along with over twenty exotic bird species and flowering plants, a gazebo and benches to relax on, cascading waterfalls and tropical trees, set to relaxing music suited perfectly for nature watching. There is a butterfly gift shop, the Wings of Imagination art gallery, and a learning center where you can explore butterfly anatomy, physiology, life cycle, feeding, and the migratory world of the royal Monarch butterfly.

Type: Attraction
Cost: $12, children $8.50, 3 and under free, seniors and military $9
When: 9:00 to 5:00, year 'round
Phone: 305-296-2988 key-westbutterfly.com

Key West Butterfly and Nature Conservatory

152

Lloyd's Tropical Bike Tour

There's nothing like riding a bike in Key West. Relax with environmentalist Lloyd Mager for a more indigenous excursion, a leisurely two-hour bike ride along streets and hidden lanes on a hands-on sensory-rich field trip. Sample tasty tropical fruits like fresh coconut, key limes, mangoes, sapodilla, Surinam cherries, or maybe sugar apples. Regardless of physical limitations, disability, or age, you will experience and learn about the lush tropical plant life, the unique styles of the homes of old Key West, an array of bird life that make their daily appearance: ospreys, hawks, frigates, pelicans, cormorants, egrets, ibis, and/or maybe a great white heron. Along the way he might stop and interview someone who's grown up here who can tell you what it was like in the "old days", or introduce you to the coolest dogs, cats or parrots. He also has access to some spectacular private gardens, such as the Japanese Medicine Garden, and Nancy's Secret Garden, an unbelievable hidden miniature rain forest right in the heart of old Key West, complete with orchids, huge stalks of bamboo, and squawking orphaned parrots that Nancy has adopted and now cares for.

151

Type: Tour
Cost: $39, includes bike rental
When: Year 'round
Phone:
305-428-2678

Located at the Moped Hospital, 601 Truman Avenue

The Annual Key West
Santa Run

Not a marathon! Not a charity! Not a race! Just as many Santas as are willing to run through the streets of Key West, drinking, bar to bar. Santas, Mrs. Santas, elves, snowmen, baby Jesus's, reindeer and Grinch's all meet up at a pre-designated bar, and then when the head Santa blows the whistle, everyone grabs their drinks and jingle bells and dashes to the next nearby bar along the pre-designated Santa route for another drink pit stop (about 15-20 minutes at each one to catch your breath). Then, the whistle blows again, and off you go! About seven or eight stops, then a party at the end. Great way to spend Christmas Eve with friends if you can't be north with family for the holidays. No sign-ups. No fees. No delivering toys. Just show up, drink, and

run, for some silly holiday fun. Sponsored by the Key West TODAY Facebook Page, should you be interested in participating.

Type: Holiday Fun
Cost: Free
When: Every
Christmas Eve

150

Key West Cemetery

It is estimated that as many as 100,000 people are buried in the Key West Cemetery, most in above-ground vaults due to the high water table, many more than the 30,000 residents who currently live on the island. There are lovely statues of angels and lambs, and a strange one of a naked, bound woman, Magdalena Yates, at the grave of her husband Archibald John Sheldon Yates. There are large family plots, Masonic lodges for all major ethnic groups: black, white, and Cuban, a monument to the USS Maine, and a Jewish Cemetery. Key West notables 'Sloppy' Joe Russell and Wilhelmina Harvey are buried there. It is the final resting place of those entwined in numerous tragedies, slave burials, brutal murders, sailors lost at sea, Civil War soldiers, Yorkshire terriers, and a pet Key Deer. Read the bizarre story of Carl Von Cosel's demented love affair with a corpse. The best way to explore it is with the Key West Cemetery Map and Self-Guided Online Tour, here: http://www.keywest-travelguide.com/key-west-cemetery-map-self-guided-tour/. Notable epitaphs you should look for: "Devoted Fan of Singer Julio Eglasias," "I'm Just Resting My Eyes,' and 'I Told You I Was Sick'.

Type: Self-guided tour
Cost: Free
When: Year 'round

149

I TOLD YOU I WAS SICK
B. P. ROBERTS
MAY 17, 1929
JUNE 18, 1979

Located in the heart of Old Town between Angela St, Frances St, Olivia St, and Windsor Lane

148

Lobsterfest

A celebration of our favorite crustacean! Every second weekend in August, from Thursday to Sunday, we celebrate the opening of Lobster Season by throwing the biggest party of the summer: Key West Lobsterfest! Thousands of lobster lovers descend on Key West for four glorious, buttery days and nights of lobster-inspired events, a Duval Street street fair with arts, crafts, beer, shots, lots and lots of locally-caught Florida lobster, and a big, free street concert that goes all night. Don't forget your bib!

Type: Event   Cost: Free   When: Thurs-Sun, 2nd Weekend in August

Street Fair Runs from the 100 Block of Duval Street to the 500 Block, and All the Side Streets in Between

*Type: Sight-
seeing/shopping
Cost: Nothing,
to watch
When: 365 days
a year*

Bikinis

147

Whether you're wearing one or watching one, they're in season all year 'round, on bikes, in stores, at the pool, at the restaurant, at the bar, on the beach, at the gym, in our wildest dreams.

146

Over 10,000 motorcycle riders traverse one of America's most scenic highways, the Overseas Highway (U.S. Highway 1), which stretches 113 miles from mainland Florida to Key West, and crosses 42 bridges - one of them nearly seven miles long - each and every September for Peterson's Key

West Poker Run. Riders stop at five places along the way to pick up poker cards, concluding at the Conch Republic Seafood Company at Greene and Elizabeth Streets. Prizes are awarded to the best poker hands. Lower Duval Street is closed to car traffic from 1 p.m. to 2 a.m. both Friday and Saturday, so bikers can park on the street to display their bikes, many rightfully called works of art. Proceeds from the event go to local charities. For more information, visit www.petersonskeywestpokerrun.com.

Bike Week

Type: Event
Cost: Free
When: Mid Sept.

Duval Street from Greene St to Southard St

Antique Shopping  145

There is a plethora of antique shops dotting the downtown landscape of Key West in between the bars, t-shirt shops and art galleries, filled with treasures from shipwrecks, estate sales and long-forgotten attics. Peruse Duval, Fleming, Petronia, and Greene Streets to begin.

Type: Shopping
Cost: ??
When: Year
'round

144 *Go Fishin'* ☐

Type: Recreation
Cost: Varies dramatically
When: Year 'round

Key West is a fisherman's paradise. There are no limits to the options available: flat fishing, backcountry fishing, light tackle fishing, offshore fishing, trolling, bottom fishing, trophy shark fishing, spearfishing, deep blue fishing, full or half-day, night fishing, overnight fishing... The only thing you'll need to bring along is something to eat and drink. Your captain takes care of everything else, from the fishing tackle to licenses, bait, ice, a first mate and crew, and of course years of Key West fishing experience. Snapper, tuna, sailfish, wahoo, marlin, Mahi-Mahi (dolphin), grouper, barracuda, tarpon, permit, kingfish, porgies, grunts, mackerel, bonefish, jacks, pompanos...just to name a few. Your crew will prepare your catch for you when you reach shore (often serving it sushi-style on the dock) and/or direct you to a nearby restaurant that will be happy to prepare your fresh catch for you for dinner. Check out boats online or just show up at the dock. Plenty of friendly faces willing to answer all your questions.

Locations: Charter Boat Row at Garrison Bight, Key West Harbor at the end of Front Street or William Street, Hurricane Hole on Stock Island

Key West ■ Shipwreck Museum

Type: Museum
Cost: $15 adults, $9 child, $13 senior, under 3 free, online discounts
When: Year 'round
Phone: 305-292-8990
keywestshipwreck.com

Enter the world of 1856 Key West, where more than a hundred ships per day passed through some of the most treacherous waters in the world. On average, at least one ship per week would wreck somewhere along the Florida Reef. Step back into time in the Key West Shipwreck Museum as you discover Key West's unique maritime heritage and how we quickly became the richest city in the United States. The museum combines actors, films and the actual artifacts from the 1985 rediscovery of the wrecked vessel Isaac Allerton, which sank in 1856 on the treacherous Florida Keys reef. Join master wrecker Asa Tift and his wrecking crew as he tells you the story of how this unusual industry provided for the livelihoods of the early pioneers of Key West. You will be invited to climb the 65' lookout tower and if need be, alarm Mr. Tift of any wrecks on the reef with the cry, "Wreck ashore!"

143

Located at 1 Whitehead Street, at Mallory Square

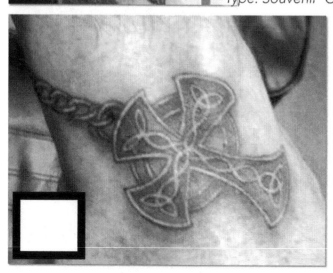

Get A
Tattoo

Type: Souvenir Cost: Around $100/hour

Take something home you can't giftwrap or put in a box. Get a one-of-a-kind tattoo. Try either Paradise Tattoo or Southernmost Tattoo, both on Duval Street, or Key West Tattoo Company on Stock Island.

142

Nancy's
Secret Garden

Just two blocks off Duval Street, pass through a magical gate and step into a jungle of centuries-old trees, ferns, vines, banana palms and beautiful orchids. Nancy Forrester, artist, teacher, and environmental activist has been rescuing orphaned parrots, South Americam macaws (four of which are critically endangered), and cockatoos, for over thirty years. From 10 to 11am daily, guests can take pictures of uncaged birds, hold them, and ask questions. Nancy gladly welcomes families with children. 11 to 3pm is self-guided tours, with educational displays that include each parrot's story.

Type: Attraction
Cost: $10 adults, $5 children, under five free
When: Year 'round
Phone:305-294-0015:

141

Located at 518 Elizabeth Street

140

Bar Wars

Type: Event
Cost: Free
When: First Sunday in August

Located at Schooner Wharf Bar on Lazy Lane

Every first Sunday in August since 1994, Schooner Wharf Bar has sponsored the Annual Battle of the Bars, a day of beer, bartenders, margaritas and costume silliness, to help improve the lives of local residents by benefitting local charities. Always at the slowest and hottest time of the year, teams from each bar or restaurant race against the clock and each other in a hilarious drunken obstacle course that fills the entire street. Each team of seven: 1. makes a margarita and hands it to 'server' who must 2. carry drink on a tray with one hand through a cone obstacle course and hand it to 3. a 'guest' who chugs it and the 4. barback grabs glass, runs it to a tub, grabs a bag of refuse, runs the length of the course and separates it into recycling bins. 5. grabs a keg, rolls it to 6. who taps keg, pours seven draft beers on a tray, and 7. walks tray of beers across balance beam to the now assembled team of seven, who must one by one chug the beer, and finish by placing empty cup upside down on their head. From 12:30pm to 6:30pm.

Kiteboarding
139

Although kiteboarding might not be for everyone, kiteboard watching certainly is. Strictly a winter sport (from late October through May), the wind conditions must also be just right for good kiting. If you're interested in giving this recreational sport a go, there are several good places to check out for instruction: beginners,

intermediate, or advanced. Try UpWind Kiteboarding or KiteHouse for more info.

Type: Water activity
Cost: Free to watch, pay for lessons
When: Late Oct. thru May

Located at Smathers Beach on S. Roosevelt Blvd.

Showers $1.00
To WATCH
$2.00

138

BLUE HE

Blue Heaven

Type: Restaurant/Photo op   Cost: Moderate
When: Year 'round   Phone: 305-296-8666

Arguably the most popular and unusual breakfast restaurant on the island, Blue Heaven also serves incredible al fresco lunches and dinners in an art deco jungle atmosphere, complete with chickens, roosters and baby chicks running about at your feet. The menu is so incredible it rarely changes. You'll want to check out their gift shop and rooster graveyard, too. Oh! And their outdoor shower! Live music most days from 11:00am till 1:00pm for lunch, and 7:00 till 9:00pm for dinner.

Located at Petronia and Thomas Streets in Bahama Village

Many of the employed musicians you now enjoy in the bars and restaurants in Key West started out as street musicians, plying the passersby for tips as they paid their dues curbside. From the silly to the sublime, you might experience a flautist playing Jethro Tull, a banjo-picking Darth Vader, or a guy pummeling out rhythms on household items such as pickle buckets and garbage can lids. Whatever the case, you can spare a dollar (or more). Help keep Key West unique. The sidewalks would be boring without them.

Type: Entertainment
Cost: At least $1
When: Year 'round

Tip a Street Musician

Located usually on Duval Street

136

Dion's Chicken

If you don't take any other advice while visiting Key West, take this. If you like fried chicken, you've got to try Dion's. Sure, it's served from a gas station convenience store. Sure, it's probably not healthy. And, sure, there are probably live chickens wandering all around the property picking up scraps off the streets, but don't let that deter you. This fried goodness has been a staple in the diets of locals for decades. Whether heading to the beach, out on a boat, after leaving the bars, or having a picnic, this chicken is fresh, juicy, tender, with a mouth-watering crunchy coating, and offers breasts nearly the size of grapefruits. You'll never look at a piece of KFC the same again. Larry R. Dion, a bomber pilot in World War II who in 1948 started a fuel company with his wife, created the first convenience stores in Key West. In the 1970s and '80s, Dion's owned twenty-five stores. Now there are just twelve from the Florida Keys to Homestead, Florida City. In the Keys: 1127 Truman Ave. at White Street, 3228 Flagler Ave., 5350 US-1 on Stock Island, and 4908 Overseas Highway on Big Coppitt Key.

Type: Food   Cost: Inexpensive   When: Year 'round

Located at Truman and White Streets

135

Walk up the 88 steps of the 100-foot historic Key West Lighthouse tower, located directly across the street from the Ernest Hemingway House on upper Whitehead Street, and search the sea beyond the edge of the land. Having been through the destruction of both war and hurricanes, the current structure which opened in 1848 offers a unique glimpse into a lifestyle long gone. The lighthouse museum features photographs, belongings and words of the lighthouse keepers and their families.

Type: Attraction/museum
Cost: Adults $10, children $5,
under six free, student and
senior discounts
When: Daily 9:30am till 4:30pm
Phone: 305-294-0012

Key West Lighthouse
Located at 938 Whitehead Street

Every year, the exuberant Goombay Street Festival officially kicks off Fantasy Fest, showcasing live music, island and African arts and crafts, dancing in the street, and delicious cultural and festival foods such as conch, lobster, alligator-on-a-stick, arepas, and exotic island desserts. The main stage is located at the corner of Petronia and Emma Streets and features non-stop musical entertainment from reggae to gospel. Just beyond that, a children's carnival with rides. It takes place over the weekend (Friday and Saturday) one week before the big Fantasy Fest Parade.

Goombay Festival

Type: Festival Cost: Free
When: Late October

134

Located on Petronia Street in Bahama Village

Snorkel the Coral Reef

133

Type: Activity Cost: $40+
When: Year 'round, but winter is nippy

A mere six miles south of Key West, in the National Marine Sanctuary, exists the only living coral barrier reef in North America, the third largest in the world. Even if you can't swim, you can snorkel, for a couple of reasons. Everything is more buoyant in salt water than in fresh water (because salt water is denser than fresh water), and you wear an inflatable life vest (if you want). No matter your age or level of experience, snorkeling, in essence, is the equivalent of lying face down on the couch and watching TV. But this TV show is observing the diverse and amazing natural ecosystem of the Florida Keys. There are more than 150 species of fish and 50 species of coral in these warm and crystalline waters. Want to change channels? Kick a little bit. There are convenient sign-up booths all over the island for tours. Try to book one that's heading to Sand Key Lighthouse, a shallow water shipwreck, or the Dry Tortugas National Park. Price may include light breakfasts or lunches, draft beer, wine, and soft drinks. Includes all equipment: mask, snorkel, fins, and safety vest. Check out Sebago Watersports, Fury Water Adventures, Sunset Watersports, or Key West Snorkeling Tours.

Located everywhere - We're on an island

Attend a Church Service

Key West might be known for how many bars it has per capita, but, surprisingly to some, there are around fifty active places of worship scattered around this little island as well, whether it be synagogues, churches or mosques: Catholic, Methodist, Buddhist, Jewish, Presbyterian, Islamic, Pentecostal, Christian Scientist, Church of Christ, Lutheran, Baptist, Hispanic Spanish, Quaker, Orthodox, Episcopal, Jehovah's Witness, Seventh Day Adventist, Latter Day Saints, Non-Denominational, and more. Google for more info. Take time to enrich the spirit.

Type: Activity
Cost: Option-
al donation
When: Year
'round

Type: Nature Cost: Free
When: 9:00 to 4:00 Mon to
Fri, 10:00 to 3:00 week-
ends, year 'round
Phone: 305-872-0774

Visit Deer Key

The endangered miniature Key deer, a subspecies of the white-tailed deer (but only the size of a large dog), lives only in the Florida Keys. They are often found in residents' yards and along roadsides, resulting in car-to-deer collisions. In 1955, population estimates ranged as low as 25. Recent estimates put the population between 700 and 800. Road kills from drivers on US 1, which traverses the deer's small range, is the major threat, averaging between 125 and 150 kills per year, 70% of the annual mortality, due to little natural fear of man or vehicles. It is not unusual to see them at dusk and dawn, from Sugarloaf Key to Bahai Honda Key, but they can easily swim between all the islands. The National Key Deer Refuge Visitor Center can be found at 179 Key Deer Blvd. on Big Pine Key.

131

☐

Big Pine Key - Around Mile Marker 30

The most visited and photographed landmark in Key West is an anchored concrete buoy marking the Southernmost Point in the continental United States. It is located at the corner of South and Whitehead Streets. Established in 1983 by the city, there is generally a short line waiting to take photos, 24 hours a day, seven days a week, 365 days a year. The nearest landfall to the south? Havana, Cuba, just 90 miles away.

130
Type: Photo op
Cost: Free
When: Year 'round

Southernmost Point

Quite simply, for so many reasons, don't drive. Space is at a premium on this tiny island and the roads weren't designed a hundred or so years ago for two cars to pass by each other, much less big trucks and SUVs. Parking is a nightmare. There are so many more practical options available: cabs, bicycle rentals, golf carts, hotel shuttles, pedicabs, and, even though scooter accidents are the most prevalent causes of injury in town, you can always get a space at the front door of just about anywhere you want to go for free. Or better yet, walk. There is so much to see that you might otherwise miss.

Type: Advice   Cost: Bikes start at $12/day
Phone for cab: 305-296-6666 (Five 6's)

Don't Drive

The all time record low in Key West is 41 degrees, set back in 1981. The hottest it's ever been was 97 degrees, set back in 1880. So, chances are, wherever you are in the world, the weather is better, summer or winter, on this little island. There are pools all over the place, but you'll want to check out Dante's, located right on the Conch Harbor Marina, next to where the Key West Express docks. Besides a large, refreshing pool frequented by locals, there's a full restaurant and either live music or DJs in the evenings. Whether soaking in a pool, or basking in the salty sea, dress and prepare appropriately. 89 degrees average temps during the summer (water temp 87) is like warm bath water, and average low 75 in the winter (water temp 69) can be quite nippy.

Swim 365 Days a Year

Type: Recreation Cost: Free, most likely When: Year 'round

Dante's Pool is where Grinnell Street hits the Harbor

127

Type: Restaurant
Cost: Moderate
When: Year 'round
Phone: 305-296-8102

☐

Better Than Sex

Release your inhibitions and captivate all your senses in the most romantic way when you finish off a perfect evening of romance at Better Than Sex, a dessert restaurant. Indulge your decadent curiosities with chocolate dipped wine, a caramel-rimmed beer or champagne, or with a cheeky-named dessert. You'll have a few giggles while you're at it. One of Key West's most captivating experiences.

Located at 926 Simonton Street, at Truman Ave

Featuring the best singer/songwriters in Key West!

Rise by Tony Roberts
Coconut Jam by Jeff Clark
My Little Island Home by Caffeine Carl
You're Harmony by Zack Seemiller
Homegrown by Cliff Cody
Local on the Eights by Howard Livingston
Problem by the Doerfels
Layin' Low by Karri Daley
Cheap Cocaine by Nick Norman
Anywhere Bound by El Dub
Talk by Kevin Poole
I Like It Hot by Dani Hoy
Home by Mike Festa and Jettison Theory
My Little Island Town by Chris Rehm
Sink or Swim by Bill Blue
Days Like These by John Taglieri
Respectfully by Anthony Picone
Square Grouper by MC COUSCOUS

The best selling compilation CD in Key West two years in a row is available in retail outlets all over the island: the Smokin' Tuna Saloon, the Conch Republic Seafood Company, Key West Island Books on Fleming, Carolyn's on Caroline, Island Dogs, the Six-Toed Cat, the Grateful Guitar and Gone Fishin' on Duval. By mail or digital download, look for 'The Best of Key West, Volumes One and Two' on CDBaby.com and iTunes. $1 from every copy sold goes to benefit the Sister Season Fund of Key West.

The Best of Key West

A compilation of great songs showcasing the diverse rock, blues, reggae, jazz and island sounds one might expect to hear while walking the streets of Key West, performed by Key West's finest songwriter/entertainers.

Featured on Volume Two:

Left Me Down in the Keys by Patrick and the Swayzees

Bleed by Joal Rush

Another Key West Night by Matt Quinton

Right Back by Tony Baltimore

Tiger by Leah Orlikowski

Mona by the Love Lane Gang

Kino Song by Bill Wharton

Duval Street by Roenin

Blue Day by Adrienne Z

Skills to Pay the Bills by Larry Baeder

Key Western Cowboy by CW Colt

The Conch Republic Song by Michael McCloud

Goodbye Captain Tony by Don Middlebrook

Seeking Peace by Mary Spear

Babylon by Jeff Clark

Souls on Ice by The MuseGurus

Feel the Scene by Bria Ansara

Devil in the Deep by Gabriel Wright

My Father's Balls/Grandpa's Nuts by Pete and Wayne

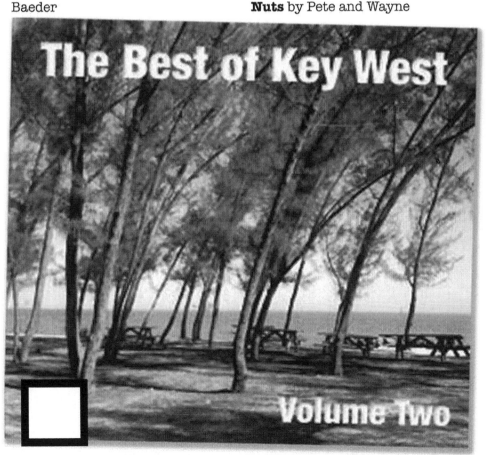

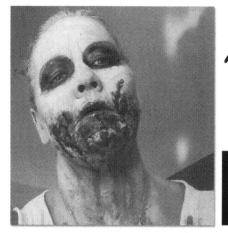

Zombie Bike Ride

The Zombie Bike Ride was created in 2009 as a kick-off to Fantasy Fest and has quickly grown from a couple hundred people to over 8,000 in 2016. The ride is a little over four miles long and takes a leisurely pace down US1 along the Atlantic Ocean with a police escort, right at sunset, past the Zombie Beach Bash at Salute' On The Beach, and eventually down to Duval Street where the ZombieFest erupts. Zombie Land at the historic and haunted Fort East Martello opens at 2pm,

126

Type: Event Cost: $5 registration fee When: Usually the third Sunday of October Phone: 305-294-7433

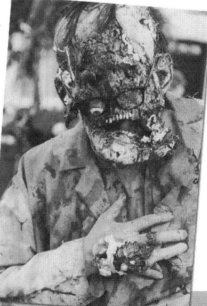

with live music, entertainment, vendors and face and body paint. Face painting is first-come first-served for usually around $10, but prices are negotiated with each individual artist. Some artists do take appointments earlier in the day. A $5 registration fee per rider pays for the insurance, street closures, cone rentals, police officers and permits, plus a souvenir Zombie Bike Ride collectable numbered sticker. The Zombie t-shirts, designed by local artist and Zombie Bike Ride creator Marky Pierson of Wonderdog Productions and Design, sell out every year. Bike rentals are available from WeCycle Bike Shop. Visit wecyclekw.com for more info.

Starts at Fort East Martello on S. Roosevelt Blvd.

Get Naked

125

☐

Type: Bar
Cost: No cover
When: Year 'round

On the rooftop of the Bull and Whistle three-plex bar, just beneath the stars and the moon, is the clothing-optional Garden of Eden Bar. It's a hike up three flights of stairs, but once you arrive, if you're in the mood, take it off. Take it all off. Full-service bar available, with a great staff. But you'll soon find out that not everyone who is naked should be naked. A lot of fun, whether you want to get involved or you're just a voyeur. No cameras allowed though, please.

Located at 224 Duval Street at Caroline

124

□

Key Lime Pie

What do you do with millions of Key limes? You make Key lime pie, that's what! There's probably not a restaurant in town that doesn't offer the World's Best. Check out Kermit's Key Lime Pie

Shoppe at the corner of Greene and Elizabeth Streets, and hang out by the koi pond. The pie pictured above, with the mile high meringue, comes from Blue Heaven restaurant on Petronia Street in Bahama Village.

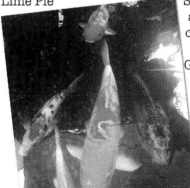

Type: Food   Cost: Couple of bucks

Located at shops and restaurants all over Key West

37

Invasion of the *Parrotheads*

Type: Weeklong event   When: Starts the last weekend of October, after Fantasy Fest

After ten days of decadence, outrageous costumes, parties, and painted naked bodies roaming the streets, in one day, from the last Saturday of October to the following Sunday morning, the entire island does an immediate 180 degrees, welcoming the Tommy Bahama-wearing, much more congenial troprock festival fanatics to the island, the Meeting of the Minds, aka Parrothead Week. Inspired originally by the greatest troprocker of all, Key West alum Jimmy Buffett, the tradition continues on yearly, with concerts, pina coladas, beads and silly hats. Is Key West actually 'Margaritaville'? Like many of his other songs, 'Caroline Street', 'A Pirate Looks at Forty', and 'Last Mango in Paris' among many others, it was definitely inspired by it. Hear great troprockers from all around the world.

Jimmy McGee the Mojito Man

122

Just a hop across the little bridge that separates Mallory Square from the Margaritaville Resort is a little mojito stand run by longtime employee Jimmy McGee. The drinks are strong, and chances are, Jimmy's going to pour you a little extra.

Type: Drink Cost: $10 When: Sunset, year 'round

Located at the Margaritaville Resort on the Pier

Bird

Naturalist John James Audubon was possibly the first to enjoy Key West birdwatching, discovering 52 types of birds new to him during his one Key West visit. The seven tiny islands of Dry Tortugas alone are a vital layover for migrating birds traveling between South America and the United States making it a staple in the Great Florida Birding Trail. The Florida Keys are a haven for wildlife since they fall within the Florida Keys National Marine Sanctuary, a 2,800 square nautical mile area surrounding the Keys and reaching into the Atlantic Ocean, Florida Bay and the Gulf of Mexico. This

Watching

Type: Activity   Cost: Free
When: Year 'round

includes even the plentiful chickens and roosters running around town underfoot (nobody owns them — they're wild!) If you keep an eye out, you may also spot doves, ruby-throated hummingbirds, redwing blackbirds, gray kingbirds, black-whiskered vireos, cormorants, laughing gulls, osprey, great egrets, brown pelicans, great white herons, great blue herons, greenback herons, shiny cowbirds, white-crowned pigeons, caribbean short-eared owls, brown-crested flycatchers, Bell's vireos, red-legged honeycreepers, sooty terns, brown noddys, black noddys, magnificent frigatebirds, masked boobys, sharpshinned and broad-winged hawks, merlins, peregrine falcons, American kestrels. belted kingfishers, gray catbirds, yellow-rumped and palm warblers, savannah sparrows, yellow billed cuckoos and white-eyed vireo. Nearly 300 species of birds have been spotted here, so get started.

121

120

□

Bananas, mangoes, coconuts, starfruit, Key limes,
avocadoes, oranges, kumquats, papaya, passion fruit...
they all grow naturally, often just a reach from a sidewalk.
However, please ask first. Otherwise, it's stealing.
Type: Food   Cost: Free   When: Year 'round

Eat from a Tree

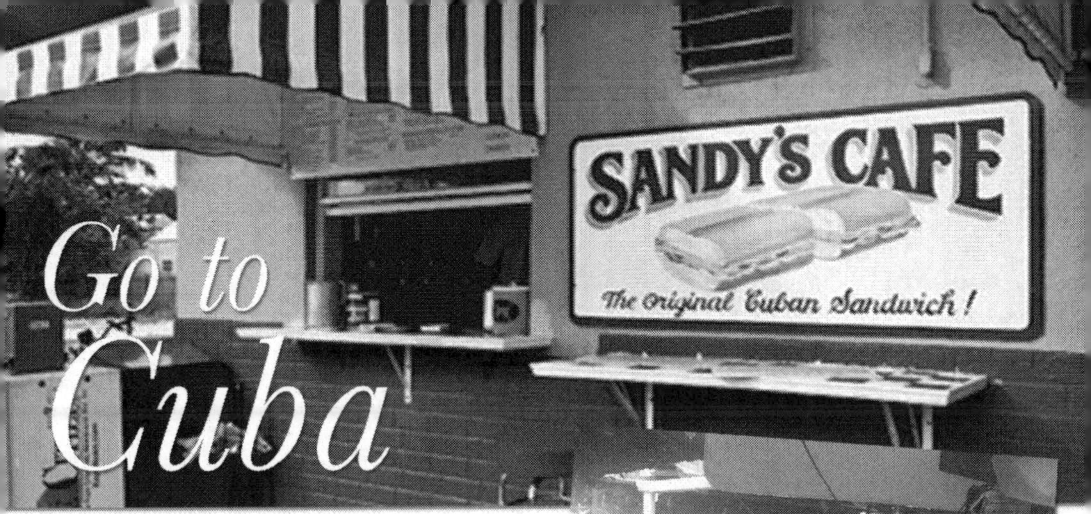

Go to Cuba

This is meant literally, since the doors have been opened recently to socialize with our friendly neighbors to the south. Or, with a rich history steeped in Cuban culture, explore the bounty of Cuba right here in Key West. Havana is a short 90 miles away to the south. Our next nearest big-city neighbor, Miami, is nearly twice that distance to the north. Have a con leche, a Cuban sandwich, ropa vieja, some rum, plantains or a cigar at any one of a number of Cuban and Cuban-inspired establishments around town.

SANDY'S CAFE
The Original Cuban Sandwich!

CUBAN COFFEE QUEEN

Type: Shopping/ food/restaurant

119

Located all over Key West

43

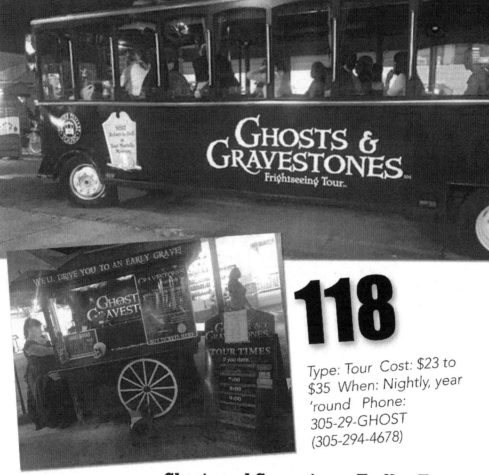

118

Type: Tour Cost: $23 to $35 When: Nightly, year 'round Phone: 305-29-GHOST (305-294-4678)

Ghosts and Gravestones Trolley Tour

Travel the narrow, dark streets of Old Town aboard the Trolley of the Doomed in search of forgotten souls, tales of murder, disease, and misfortune. Search for lost tombs, strange dolls, and the Lady in Blue, stories so tragic, so chilling, you'll see why the Travel Channel has identified Key West as one of America's "Most Haunted" locations, ranking it fourth of the ten most haunted cities in the country by Haunted America Tours. Tour one of the island's haunted Civil War forts - once quarantine barracks for suffering soldiers left to die from yellow fever; now home to Robert the Doll, who some say can play tricks on you if you don't play nicely. Hosts add a pinch of humor to tales of deathly love, tragic endings, scores to settle, wrongs to right and ghastly folk – some so strange it will be hard to believe they're true. Tour Length: 1 hour and 30 minutes. Reservations are required.

Located at 501 Front Street at Duval - Conch Train Depot

Hunt for Ghosts

Haunted Key West - Three Old Town Walking Tours

Sloan's Key West Ghost Hunt - Who haunts the bell tower at St. Paul's Church? Which famous building was built on top of a burial ground? Why do the children's spirits refuse to leave the old theater? Meet at 9:15pm at Kelly's Bar, Grill & Brewery, 301 Whitehead Street. Tours last about 90 minutes and finish inside a haunted saloon's secret 'brothel room'. Can you brave the haunted wheelchair?

Haunted Happy Hour Saloon Stroll - Stroll includes outlaw ghosts, bizarre murders, & maritime spirits. All participants must be 21 or older & have valid ID. Drinks include draft beer, house wine, or house rum drink at three bars and rum from the still at the haunted distillery. Meet at 3:30pm at Lagerheads Beach Bar, 0 Simonton Street.

Infamous Hauntings Ghost Tour - Tour includes Ernest Hemingway, the haunted lighthouse, Typhoid Mary, and a murdered Klansman. Meet at 7:15pm at Gone Fishin!, 1102 Duval Street. Reservations are required.

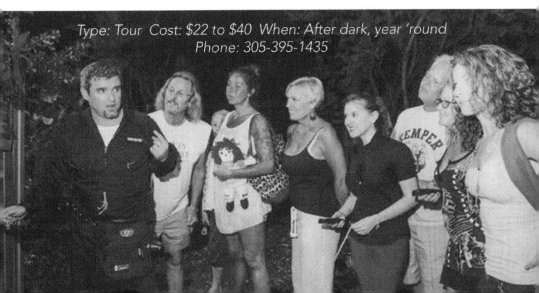

Type: Tour Cost: $22 to $40 When: After dark, year 'round
Phone: 305-395-1435

Type: Event Cost: Free
When: First week in
November

Powerboat Races

Everyone in town knows when it's powerboat week in Key West. The sound reverberates and rattles windows all across the island. The most powerful boats in the world, along with thousands of avid fans, surge into town for a spectacle unlike any other in November - the Super Boat International. It's no mean feat even on a good day, plying this oblong race course, close to six miles in length, but generally the waters here are anything but calm this time of year. That's just how they like it. The rougher the water gets, the faster they go, up to 200mph. Helicopters overhead add to the deafening wall of sound and excitement. This year will mark the 30th anniversary of the World Championships in Key West, Fla.

117

Key West Brewfest

For the beer lovers! More than 150 beers and micro-brews are on tap at this tasty annual event that benefits the charitable efforts of the Key West Sunrise Rotary Club of the Conch Republic. Events from beer dinners, beer brunches, happy hour parties, pool parties, late-night parties, seminars and the Signature Tasting Festival Event are some of the offered activities.

116

Type: Event Cost: Depends on how much beer you drink When: First week of September, around Labor Day Phone: 305-295-6519 keywestbrewfest.com

Parasailing

To get dipped or not to get dipped, that is the question. One of the most exciting and yet tranquil experiences you can have is to be whisked off into the sky out above the beautiful tropical colors of our crystal clear waters. It is remarkably peaceful and quiet. You can see for miles in all directions, and can often spot sea turtles or manatees below. The Fury, Sunset Watersports, and Sebago are all trusted companies, but there are many others on both sides of the island, and you'll find them all to be reputable and accomodating. TIP: Choose an all-day or half-day adventure, and they'll throw in jet-skiing, snorkeling the coral reef, floating waterslide/bouncy houses, kayaks, food, and beverages, including beer and wine, after you're done and ready to relax. This is one water activity where it's possible to stay completely dry, if you should so choose. TIP TWO: Bring some sunscreen.

Type: Activity Cost: Starts around $40 per person When: Year 'round

Located at Key West Harbor and on Smathers Beach

Dominique
and his Amazing
Trained Housecats

No trip to Key West would be complete without experiencing Dominique the Catman. Shaggy-maned Dominique LeFort mixes mime, posed dance postures, and outrageous French-accented commands to both his enthralled audience and to his feline cohorts. He has been performing for audiences nightly

Type: Entertainment Cost: Tips When: An hour before sunset, year 'round

during Key West Sunset Celebrations on Mallory Square since 1981. Dominique and his amazing cats offer a unique show that is as sensational as it is silly.

114 ▢

113

Type: Activity/
Tour Cost: $47
adults, $24 child
When: Year
'round, departure
times vary Phone:
888-976-4338

Glass Bottom Boat

Experience Key West's vi-
brant underwater paradise
without ever having to get
wet on the Glass Bottom Boat
& Sunset Cruise Reef Eco
Tour aboard a 65ft state-of-
the-art catamaran glass
bottom boat. With an air-conditioned viewing area, twin
45-degree observation hulls
and a large seated sundeck,
view North America's only
living coral reef in dry com-
fort, along with your expert
tour guide. Who knows, you

might even spot a
sea turtle or a
stingray! Enjoy
snacks, compli-
mentary beverag-
es, and a cham-
pagne toast just as
the sun sets.

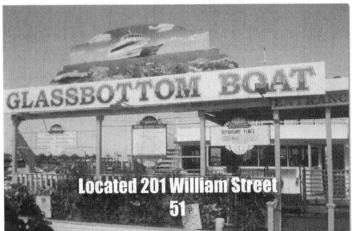

Located 201 William Street
51

112

Moderate

Yes, it's a party town. Just moderate. You don't want to wake up in the morning on the sidewalk. Or worse.

Key West Lighted Christmas Boat Parade

After an evening of Christmas shopping, holiday music, dinner and drinks, kick off the holiday season at the Historic Seaport with the Key West Lighted Boat Parade. Between twenty and thirty hand-decorated boats loop the shimmering harbor to the delight of all. This year marks the 26th Annual.

Type: Event Cost: Free When: Saturday night, mid-December, around 8:00pm Phone: 305-292-3302 Schooner Wharf

Located at Schooner Wharf Bar and the Harbor Walk of Lights

110 *Minimal Regatta at Schooner Wharf*

Construction Rules:
1. One sheet of 4' x 8' x 1/4" plywood
2. Two 2" x 4" x 8's
3. One pound of fasteners
4. One roll of 2" x 60 yard duct tape
5. No caulking or adhesives - Epoxy paint is permitted
6. Painting of boats is optional

Each six member team must build a vessel seaworthy enough to stay afloat for the duration of the race course. Many do not, sending them overboard into the drink.

Type: Event Cost: Free to watch When: Sunday in late May Phone: 305-292-3302 Schooner Wharf

There are two categories: Kayak/Canoe, and Open Design, with 1st and 2nd place prizes for the Fastest, the Most Creative, the Best Paint Job, the Best Costumed Entry, Sportsmanship and the coveted Sinker Award, which is always a crowd pleaser.

Located at the Key West Bight at Schooner Wharf Bar

Truman's Little White House

Arriving here in 1946, the Harry S. Truman Little White House was the winter White House for President Harry S. Truman for 175 days during eleven visits during his presidency. Today regular guided tours take visitors through the site, and one can enter the rooms where the Trumans lived, worked, and relaxed. His briefcase, books, telephone, and his famous "The Buck Stops Here" sign are still at his desk.

Type: Attraction/Museum Cost: Online $15 adult, $4.50 youth, $13 seniors, kids and locals free. When: Year 'round, opens daily 9:00 to 4:30 Phone: 305-294-9911 trumanlittlewhite-house.com

THE LITTLE WHITE HOUSE

Built in 1890 as quarters for Navy officers, the Little White House later was used by American Presidents William Howard Taft, Harry S. Truman, Dwight Eisenhower, John F. Kennedy, Jimmy Carter, and Bill Clinton. Truman used the facility as a vacation home and functioning White House between 1946 and 1952. National legislation was drafted and official government business was conducted daily from the site. Perhaps the most important of these actions occurred on December 5, 1951, when Truman enacted a Civil Rights executive Order requiring federal contractors to hire minorities. The house is considered the birthplace of the U.S. Department of Defense. As a result of the Key West Accords of 1948, afterdent Eisenhower used the site in 1956 while recuperating from a heart attack. In 1961, the house was the venue for a summit between President Kennedy and British Prime Minister Harold Macmillan during the Bay of Pigs incident. Kennedy returned in 1962 after the Cuban Missile Crisis. Secretary of State Colin Powell and foreign leaders held an international summit here in 2001. The Little White House was listed on the National Register of Historic Places in 1974.

*Skydive***108**

Experience the thrill of falling at speeds of 120 mph or more over the scenic bluegreen water of the Keys, and then once your parachute opens, your dive becomes peacefully quiet, and you enjoy a five to seven minute ride floating quietly back to earth for a soft, pinpoint landing. Skydive Key West has many years of experience with over 5000 skydives.

Type: Activity Cost: $225 to $265 When: Year 'round, seven days a week 9:00 to 5:00 Phone: 305-396-8806

Located at 5 Bat Tower Road, near MM 17, Sugarloaf Key

Stand Up Paddleboard

Type: Activity Cost: Rentals start at $30 When: Year 'round, weather permitting

Half kayak, half surfboard, stand up paddleboarding is one of the newest water activity crazes. Glide through the mangrove forests with an eco group, explore the open shoreline on your own or with friends, or try paddleboard yoga at dawn. Many hotels offer lessons, and some party boats provide them along with other activities. Try SUP Key West Stand Up Paddleboard Eco Tours at 305-240-1426, or Lazy Dog Stand Up Paddlebord at 305-295-9898. They both are conveniently located right across Cow Key Bridge on nearby Stock Island. No experience is necessary for paddleboarding.

Nick Doll Photography

Type: Nature   When: Always

Build a treehouse! Not really. But for anyone who ever dreamed of living in a Swiss Family Robinson-style treehouse, these are the trees you would've wanted. As they grow, they produce aerial roots that hang down from horizontal branches and take root in other branches, or where they touch the ground, creating living jungle gyms. Banyan can get 100' tall, and with their massive limbs supported by prop roots, they spread over an area of several acres. Also look for gumbo limbo trees (known as 'tourist trees' because their bark is red and always peeling), or the fan-rooted Kapok trees, (right). Check them out. Easy box to check off.

Key West Pet Masquerade

105

Dogs, cats, turtles, birds, fish... On the Wednesday of Fantasy Fest week, costumed animals and their owners join together to strut their stuff for a worthy cause, the Lower Keys Friends of Animals. More than 2000 people cheer over sixty entries as children and adults walk, dance and even skateboard across the stage with their favorite variety of pet or pets dressed in every costume imaginable. Judged in four catego ries: junior, most exotic, pet/owner lookalike, and best theme adaption. 1st, 2nd and 3rd prizes are awarded in each category, plus one grand prize winner. PetMasquerade@hotmail.com

Type: Event Cost: Free to watch, $25 per category to register (enter your pet in as many as you wish) When: The last Wednesday of October 5:30pm

Located at the Casa Marina Resort, 1500 Reynolds Street

104

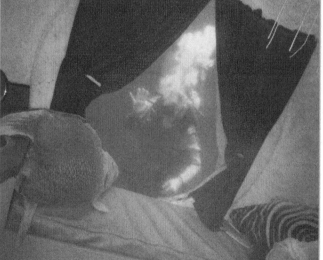

Type: Activity Cost: $800 for two (plus $100 if staying in separate quarters). 3 to 4 people, $350 each. 5 to 6 people, $300 each. One person $675. Ultimate romantic getaway for two $1395. When: Year 'round, but call for operating hours Phone: 305-451-2353 jul.com

Sleep in an □ *Underwater Hotel*

Check this one off your bucket list! Located in the lagoon at Key Largo Undersea Park, Jules' Undersea Lodge is the only underwater hotel in the Keys. To enter the Lodge, one must actually scuba dive 21 feet beneath the surface of the sea, and enter through an opening in the floor of the lodge. Diving through the tropical mangrove habitat of the Emerald Lagoon is quite an experience. Even from the outside, Jules' big 42 inch round windows cast a warm invitation to come in and stay a while, relax and get to know the underwater world that so few of us have even visited. The cottage-sized building isn't short on creature comforts, either: hot showers, a well-stocked kitchen (complete with refrigerator and microwave), books, music, and video movies. And of course there are cozy beds, where guests snuggle up and watch the fish visit the windows of their underwater "terrarium". Pizza delivery is available -- it arrives via a scubadiver delivery person, warm and hot! In addition to overnight stays in the Lodge, the Park offers a great SCUBA training location in its Lagoon, with a depth of up to 30' in a protected setting. Individuals can get Open Water certified here, do a Discover SCUBA Diving course, or just dive around in the lagoon. Some of their distinguished visitors include Aerosmith's Steve Tyler, actor Tim Allen, and former Canadian Prime Minister Pierre Trudeau! Once in a lifetime experience.

51 Shoreland Drive, Key Largo

"*Everything $5!*"

Not every one of the numerous t-shirt shops on Duval and adjacent streets are fronts for Eastern European mafia money laundering, but even those that are sell everything, EVERYTHING, inside for $5. It's an easy way to stock up on tacky, offensive, political, politically incorrect, redneck, and souvenir Key West t-shirts, gift items and paraphernalia for next to nothing. And before you back up a truck to start loading everything in the store for just $5, what they really mean is everything in the store is $5 EACH.

Type: Shopping Cost: $7. Just kidding.

Located mostly up and down Duval Street, but also on Front Street near Mallory Square where the cruise ships dock

When the fishing boats pull in with a load of fish and begin cleaning them on the pier, it's an all out war for scraps between the tarpon, jacks and pelican. Tarpon, a relative to carp and goldfish, reach 4–8 feet in length and weigh 60–280 lbs. They are sought by sportfishermen because of their fight, but they're too bony to eat. They can be seen swimming in schools all along the Harbor Walk, from A&B Lobster House up to Half Shell Raw Bar, and for pocket change there are fish food dispensaries for you and the kids to entice them to the surface. There are public tarpon feedings scheduled at noon and 4:00pm at the Key West City Marina at Garrison Bight, and 4:00pm feedings just outside Alonzo's Oyster Bar near the Conch Republic Seafood Company at the Key West Harbor. Come be amazed at the size of our big, wild, harbor pet 'goldfish'.

Feed the Tarpon
102

Type: Activity/Nature   Cost: Free to watch, pocket change to feed   When: Year 'round

Located at Garrison Bight and at the Key West Harbor

Key West has the best cops in the country. Everyone realizes it's a tourist economy and that things get a little crazy down here. Open-carry drinks are illegal, but just like jaywalking, if you don't do anything stupid, you'll probably be okay. Thank a police dog if you see one, too. They must go crazy sniffing that aromatic contraband.

101

Type: Advice   When: Year 'round

Thank a
Key West
Cop

Every April during the annual Conch Republic Independence Celebration, captivated spectators gather to witness the Great Conch Republic Drag Race, a madcap marathon designed to showcase drag stars instead of drag-sters. The contest's challenges include navigating an obstacle course of automobile tires, walking a balance beam, and maneuvering souped-up shopping carts. Thousands of spectators line the street to watch the "girls" sprint and stagger through the course while trying to avoid stumbling or breaking a heel.

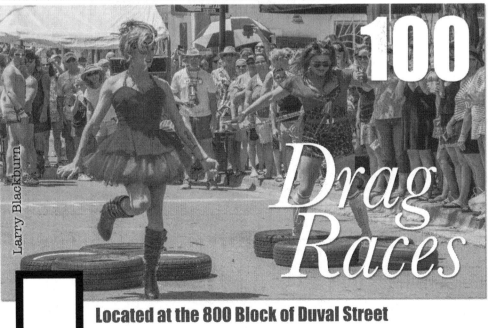

Larry Blackburn

100
Drag Races

Located at the 800 Block of Duval Street

99

Type: Activity Cost: Free
When: Year round

Is it legal? No. Do we recommend you try it? Absolutely not. Is it popular with locals? Very. The Jumping Bridge on Lower Sugarloaf Key is right off US1 at MM17 on Sugarloaf Blvd. When the road takes a sharp right, you will see a yellow barrier. People park there and walk past the yellow fence barrier to the bridge. The water is about 15 – 20 feet deep and full of fish. Watch out for boats! They use the channel. Watch for broken glass, too. Sometimes the tide is pretty strong, one way or the other, depending on where the moon is.

NO JUMPING OR DIVING FROM BRIDGE
F.S.316.130(17)

Photos by Nick Doll

Bridge Jumping

Pamper **98** *Your* *Poochie*

Key West loves its dogs. You'll see them being walked everywhere, and in some cases, they're allowed inside many outdoor bars. There are water bowls at the entrances of many businesses, and boxes of plastic poop bags mounted all over town. They have their own designated Doggie Beach at 1500 Vernon Avenue, right next door to Louie's Backyard, for romping in the sea. At Higgs Beach Doggie Park, 100 Atlantic Blvd., they can run and play off-leash at this fenced-in dog park, which includes a separate area for small pooches, grassy open spaces, shade, and benches for their people. Well-behaved, leashed pets are welcome at the picnic areas and the fort at Fort Zachary Taylor State Park at 601 Howard England Way, the local's favorite beach. Just please clean up after.

Type: Love Cost: Love is free
When: Year 'round

Located everywhere

Key West *Fishing* Tournament

97

☐

Type: Activity
Cost: Inquire
When: April 7 to
Novenmber 30
Phone: 305-295-6601

Fishermen young and old
angle for around forty species
of Florida fish, making this eight
month tournament one of the most
popular Florida Keys fishing events.
Participants are broken down by divisions for men, women, junior anglers
(ages 10 to 14) and Pee Wees (under 10
years old). Starting with the kickoff in
April, Florida Keys sport fishermen are
awarded certificates detailing catches and
cash prizes. 2017 Florida Keys Fishing
Tournaments Calendar: http://www.florida-keys-vacation.com/Florida-Keys-Fishing-Tournaments.html#ixzz4UvwLv3DR
Email: director@keywestfishingtournament.com

Located in Key West, Islamorada, Key Largo, Marathon, Tavernier and Big Pine Key

96

The big red Custom House currently serves as one of three Key West Museums of Art & History. Exhibits include local history, famous personalities including Ernest Hemingway, maritime history, and works by local artists. Because of its size, location and bright color, it is one of the most identifiable structures in Key West by air.

Type: Museum
Cost: Free
When: 9:30am to 4:30pm, year 'round
Phone: 305-295-6616

Custom House and Old Post Office

Located at 281 Front Street

95

Sponge Market
and Shell Warehouse

Key West's economy once thrived off the industry of sponging. The Key West Sponge Market is a historical shopping experience that features a museum of the sponging industry and native sponge trading, which used to fuel the livelihood of many Key West locals. Browse through the Sponge Market's ample selection of natural sponges, nautical gifts such as sea shells and shark jaws, Key West collectibles, local art, books, Key Lime products and tropical apparel.

Type: Shopping
When: Year 'round

400 Wall Street at Mallory Square

Fort East Martello Museum

94

Type: Museum
Cost: $10 adults, $5 kids, toddlers under 5 free, student and senior discounts. When: 9:30 to 4:30, year round. Phone: 305-296-3913

Photo by Rob O'Neal

While the majority of Key West citizens supported the Confederacy, Key West remained a Union-controlled island during the Civil War. In 1862, the U.S. Army built this Civil War Fort in order to provide extra protection for Key West and defend against the possibility of a Confederate sea assault. In 1950, the Key West Art & Historical Society opened the battlement as its first museum. Visitors can explore relics from the Civil War, learn about the wrecking and cigar-manufacturing industries, view the imaginative metal sculptures of Stanley Papio, as well as meet the Ghosts of East Martello, including the infamous and sometimes vindictive Robert the Doll.

Located at 3501 S. Roosevelt Blvd.

71

93

Take a Selfie with a Celebrity

Past, present and future, celebrities love our island as much as we do. There's a good chance someone's in town today. When you see them, please be polite.

© Jeff Lange 2013

Type: Event   Cost: $5 registration
When: Early April   CowKeyBridgeRun.com

KEY WEST TO STOCK ISLAND   ZER

The Zero-K
Cow Key Bridge Run

The only zero-K bridge run. Ever. Dress up or don't. This is one of the shortest bridges in the Keys and there is a party with beer after the finish line. Park. Mingle and graze with the herd. Start. Finish. Party. Held in early April during the Conch Republic Independence Celebration. There are awards.

Located on the bridge that separates Key West from Stock Island

91

Celebrate New Year's Eve

The second busiest week in Key West is the week between Christmas and New Year's. Come and revel at the Sloppy Joe's Conch Shell Drop, the Schooner Wharf Pirate Wench Drop, or with Sushi the drag queen at the Bourbon Street Red Slipper Drop, featured annually on CNN.

Type: Event
Cost: Oh, those hotels
When: New Year's Eve

90

Type: Advice
Cost: $35 up
to over $150
When: Year
'round, call
for hours

Don't let hangovers, dehydration, or low energy ruin your day. Experienced medical professionals offer both IV and injection therapies on call, rapidly curing hangovers, dehydration, and vitamin deficiencies, at your hotel room, house, office, or boat. Or, if you prefer, relax in full body massage chairs while receiving IV fluids, vitamins, oxygen and medications, providing relief for a multitude of common ailments. Restore hydration, decrease inflammation, get an energy boost, relieve stomach pain, relieve nausea & vomiting, boost immune system with a B-12 booster shot or super vitamin B-complex injection, electrolytes, anti-nausea and anti-headache medicine, antioxidants, and/or oxygen therapy. Call **Hangover Hospital** (305) 912-4911 for on sight, or **IVs in the Keys** at 531 Whitehead Street 305-395-8245 for your in-house or delivery therapy, and get back out there with vim and vigor.

Hangover Allies

Located wherever you're located

Attend an AA Meeting

86

Type: Advice

Cost: Donate a little if you'd like

When: Every evening 5:30 and again at 8:30 year 'round

Specifically encouraged for anyone who thinks they don't need it. For many, this is like church. It's an introspective and cathartic look at one-self through the stories of others. Participate if you choose, or just listen. It takes an hour, but it's hard not to be moved. On an island where the favorite pasttime is drinking and other mind-altering activities, it's refreshing every once in awhile to take a step back and gauge where these vices have fit into your life. Often you'll find yourself surprised that they've crept in a little bit further than you thought. No one judges, everything remains anonymous. They ask that if you've been drinking or doing any drugs that day that you kindly refrain from attending. Every evening at 5:30 and again at 8:30. Everyone welcome. Coffee available.

Located at Anchors Aweigh, 404 Virginia Street, at Whitehead

Type: Theater Cost: Ticket, plus
concessions (Tropic offers mem-
berships for discounted rates)
When: Year 'round
Tropic : 305-295-9493
Regal: 844-462-7342

88

□

Catch a Flick

You have two choices for moviegoing in Key West. Regal Cinemas,
the large sixplex at the top of the island, or the art deco Tropic
Cinema located downtown, which offers beer, wine (by the glass or
bottle), champagne, brie and Camembert cheese, Ghirardelli chocolate and other gourmet snacks and candies, along with real
butter popcorn with an array of specialty seasonings.

Tropic Cinema at 416 Eaton Street
Regal Cinema at 3338 N. Roosevelt in Searstown

White Street Pier

87

Type: Escape
Cost: Free
When: Anytime

...is now formally the Edward B. Knight Pier. Whether you're a pole fisherman, a dog walker, a bicyclist, a fan of sunrises, a fan of sunsets, a stormwatcher, a jogger, or you just like watching all the fish swim by, this is the spot for you. Peaceful and with benches, it is also the home of the poignant and emotionally touching Key West AIDS Memorial.

Key West
A I D S
Memorial

Located where White Street Hits the Atlantic

Type: Activity Cost: For two (or one): 15-18 minutes $199.99, 30-35 minute Island and Reef Tour $349.99, 30-35 minute Sunset Flight $429.99 When: Year 'round Phone: 305-851-UFLY (8359)

Take a Biplane Ride

Enjoy a narrated air tour of Key West from the open cockpit of a pristine 1942 UPF-7 Waco Biplane. Flying at a mere 500 feet, you might see sharks, rays, dolphin and

the occasional manatee. As you fly over and around the island, you'll see historic points of Key West, the Sand Key Lighthouse, underwater shipwrecks, and the majestic coral reef, with a DVD of your flight experience available. In operation since 1987, Raymond Cabanas is a

5th Generation Conch (over 150 years in Key West), a second generation pilot, and the current Commanding General of the Conch Republic Air Force. See the colors and charms of Key West from the intimate persective of a passing seabird in the sky.

Located at the Key West International Airport

Audubon House

and

Tropical Gardens

□ **85**

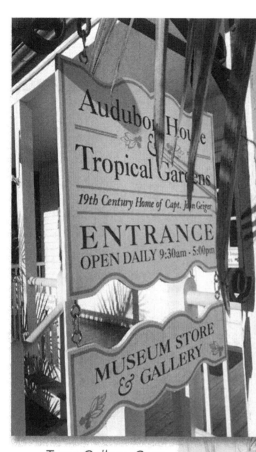

Type: Gallery Cost: Adults $14, students $10, children $5, under six FREE When: 9:30 to 5:00pm year 'round Phone: 305-294-2116

The Audubon Gallery offers a selection of original John James Audubon-Havell engravings, a selection of 500 original Audubon octavos, and 19th century lithographs of botanical and marine subjects, charts, maps, and periodical prints relevant to Florida, the Keys, Cuba and the West Indies of the 1800's.

205 Whitehead Street

Photo by Nick Doll

Get a Tutu

If there is one piece of indispensable costume attire one must have in Key West that will magically turn anything you're wearing into an automatic door-opening winner ensem, it's a simple, basic tutu. When there are parties where costumes are the only requirement, slip it on over your bikini, your burqa, your three piece suit, and you're in the door. Locals wear them all the time, just for the hell of it. Most have several to choose from, just in case. One of the biggest Fantasy Fest parties each October is the Tutu Tuesday parties where the tutu is the only requirement, but the costumes, going by each year's chosen themes, run from the bizarre to the risque to the outrageous. The good thing is -- guys or girls, one size fits all. For sale at multiple locations around town. Try Fairvilla Megastore on Front Street, and shop for adult toys and a zillion other fantastic costumes while you're at it.

Type: Advice Cost: $6 - $10 Phone: 305-292-0448

Located at 524 Front Street

83 *Bed Races* □

The Key West Bed Race is a highlight of the 10-day Conch Republic Independence Celebration held in late April each year. Each bed, mounted on wheels, is either pushed or pulled up Duval Street by four race-team members while an additional team member gets a free ride. Presented by the Bour-bon St. Pub Complex, the race is a fundraiser for the Florida Keys' AIDS Help organization and is now in its 33rd year. "The most fun you can have in bed with your clothes on."

Photos by Larry Blackburn

Type: Event Cost: Free to watch
When: During the week of the Conch Republic Independence Celebration
mid- April Phone: 305-296-0213

All the Way Down Duval Street

A revolution is coming...

After having to put a friend's beloved dog down when he turns on his master, things in Key West begin getting exponentially worse. Over the next few months, the veterinary clinic where Bill Aldrin works becomes overwhelmed with pets that have, for whatever reason, become feral and vicious, and can no longer be kept. On the news, it seems to be happening everywhere, but not just domesticated animals in homes and on farms, but in the wild as well, from giant whales to tiny microorganisms. Then, when it becomes apparent that all the animals around the world have turned on mankind, Key West veterinarian William 'Buzz' Aldrin loses all communication with his son Chase right after news breaks out that the animals in the nearby Louisville Zoo have been released by an eco-terrorist group, and are now on the loose. In a rickety motorhome with his daughter, his dog Max, and a few wary friends, he leaves his home in the Florida Keys as a hurricane approaches and battles his way north to Kentucky to hopefully locate and save his son before it's too late, as the world around them begins collapsing. It appears that man may be the next species on earth facing certain extinction, unless they can find some safe haven to escape this terrifying annihilation, or someone can find a cure.

FALL 2017

Join the 'Animal Kingdom - The Extinction Virus' Facebook page for updates, teasers, and news.

Get a Workout In

Old Town Fitness 1010 Truman Avenue
305-292-3999 Daily $15 Weekly $50

KW 24-Hour Fitness Center
725 Caroline St. 305-916-5500
Daily $20-$25 Weekly $75-$105

Everybody drinks a lot in Key West, but you'd be surprised how health-conscious they are. Take time for a walk, swim, bike ride, or a run. The stretch along Smathers Beach is a perfect spot to put in a couple of miles, right beside the Atlantic Ocean. Health clubs offer daily and weekly rates, from the more old school, no A/C, Rocky Balboa-style Old Town Fitness, to the more updated and comfortable Body Zone and the new Key West 24-Hour Fitness Center. Check online for complete list of rates.

Type: Activity
When: Year 'round
Cost: Free, or hit a gym

82

Body Zone 2740 N. Roosevelt next to Ross Dress for Less 305-292-2930
Daily $14, Weekly $60

Watch the Moon Rise
on the Afterdeck at Louie's Backyard

Type: Restaurant Cost: Fine dining
When: Open from 11:30am till 1:00am
Reservations requested Phone 305-294-1061

Overlooking the Atlantic Ocean in an historic wooden two-story building with astounding architecture sits one of Key West's finest restaurants: Louie's Backyard. The cuisine is gourmet Caribbean American, with a tapas bar on Louie's Upper Deck. Come have a bottle of wine on the romantic Afterdeck and watch the moon rise out over the sea, while experiencing the only (mild) crashing breakers on the island.

81 ◻

Experience a Good

80

Key West

Swimming in the streets!

ThunderStorm

Suddenly they come out of nowhere.

Primordial downpours.

Cars underwater!

Three feet deep in the streets.

Type: Experience

Beware open cuts --

sewer drains at street level

may cause staph infections!

Kayaks and jet skis going down Duval street.

The Best Flooding is on Front Street between Duval and Simonton

Re-enact the ancient wrecking tradition of 1800's Key West in one of the Schooner Wharf Bar Wrecker's Cup Race Series, a ruthless seven-mile one-way race from Key West Harbor to Sand Key to 'claim the booty'. The awards ceremony and party is held at 7:00 p.m. each Sunday of the race day. Trophies and prizes are earned by the top three vessels in six classes — schooner, multi-hull, classic, monohull under thirty feet, monohull 30-39 feet, and monohull forty and over. At the race start Key West harbor is a magnificent sight, filled with colorful sails and spinnakers on vessels ranging from 16 to 120 feet. You don't need a boat of your own to participate, book passage and crew on one of the charter boats in the wreckers' fleet. Log on to SchoonerWharf.com for race schedules; 2017 Race Dates are Sunday, January 29 - February 26 - March 26 and April 30.

The Schooner Wharf
Wrecker's Race

Type: Event Cost: Free to watch When: Check schedule
Phone: 305-292-3302

☐

Type: Food/drink
Cost: Couple of bucks
When: Year 'round

The Best
Coffee
in the World

Is there really a 'World's Best Cup of Coffee'? Sure, why not. But then you're into opinions. You should not leave Key West without trying a high voltage Cuban Con Leche from Cuban Coffee Queen (two locations: 284 Margaret Street, and at 5 Key Lime Square downtown) opening at 6:30am. Or Sandy's at 1026 White Street. But for the best honest-to-goodness coffee in Key West, you can't get better than Coffee Plantation at 713 Caroline Street. Each location comes with their own delicious menu items. Coffee Plantation also displays rotating art exhibits by favorite Key West artists.

77

Seven-Mile Bridge Run

One bridge, ninety minutes, 6.8 miles, 1500 runners. The Seven-Mile Bridge Run is the only known run that is completely surrounded by water from start to finish. This year is the 36th Annual 7-Mile Bridge Run, taking place April 1st. At 6:45am the bridge closes to traffic, 7:20 the race starts, and then the bridge reopens to traffic at 9:00am. Entry fee $75, proceeds go to children's organizations. There are accommodations and shuttles available. Lots of divisions, awards, and refreshments served after the race. To register, book your spot long in advance: 7MBRun.com.

Type: Event Cost: $75 registration When: Early April
Contact: 7MBRun.com

Marathon -- between Knight's Key and Little Duck Key

Key West Express

76

Type: Activity Cost: Starts at $125 round trip
When: Year 'round Phone: Call 239-463-5733 or
KeyWestExpress.net to see departure and arrival
times and discounted rates for seniors and kids

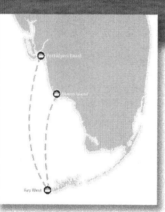

There's nothing better than slicing through the Gulf waters on a fast ferry to and from Key West and Ft. Myers Beach (and on select days to Marco Island during the winter high season). It's faster than driving and cheaper than flying. Enjoy air-conditioned interiors, exterior sun decks, couches, tables, and reclining airline-style seating. There's even a full-service galley, full-service bar, and flat screen TVs with satellite television to watch during the duration of the ride. Details at KeyWestExpress.net.

Dock at 100 Grinnell Street at the Harbor

75

Type: Theater
event Cost:
Around $20,
plus tips
When: Sponta-
neous

Burlesque is alive
and well in Key West,
but you've got to
keep an eye out for
performance dates.
'Key West Burlesque'
just celebrated ten
years of striptease in
the Florida Keys, and
might appear any-
where, at the Key
West Theater, a
restaurant, or out on
the Ocean Key
Resort Sunset Pier.
'Burlesque at 801'
has been entertain-
ing Key West for four
seasons, and runs on
the last Monday of
January, March and
May, at 9:00 and
11:00. Come enjoy
classic and neo-Bur-
lesque with a side of
comedy, live singing
and dancing. There
are no rules to these
raucous variety
shows which feature
favorite local per-
formers, exotic
guests, as well as in-
credible Key West ce-
lebrities as your
hosts. Find both
troupes on Facebook
for performance up-
dates.

Burlesque

Photo by Rob O'Neal

Photo by Nick Doll

Horseshoe crabs, lionfish, barracuda, manatees, heron, pelican, anoles, geckos, iguana, dolphin, tarpon, turkey vultures, sea turtles, ibis, Key deer, parrotfish, eels, jacks, parrotfish, nurse sharks, rays... You can't walk along the water's edge without seeing some wonder of nature. In some rare cases, you can see something truly unique like a saltwater crocodile, raccoon, flamingo, bald eagle, or a grouper the size of a Volkswagon bug. You just need to be patient and keep an eye out. They're out there.

Wildlife

Peruse An
Art Gallery

For over 200 years artist's have been selling their work in Key West, and today the number of galleries rival the number of bars. From the famous to the obscure, the whimsical to the sublime, be inspired and amazed by these heavenly creations. And if you're looking to make an investment, splurge. Walk through. Talk to the art dealers and the artists. Be enriched.

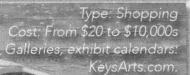

Type: Shopping
Cost: From $20 to $10,000s
Galleries, exhibit calendars:
KeysArts.com.

72

Circle the entire island on a 90-minute guided tour through the scenic Key West backcountry, visit remote islands, view famous Mallory Square and the Southernmost Point from the sea, stop and walk on a sand bar, visit the abandoned submarine pens, and maybe even spot dolphins, sea turtles or tropical birds along the way as you captain your own jet ski, solo or with a partner, beginner or expert. Most oceanside hotels offer jet ski services, and if not, there are many to choose from, ranging from $100 to $140. Some offer an hour to yourself within a three or four square mile play area on the sea. You can't go wrong with **Fury Water Adventures** (888) 976-0899, departing from five locations: Westin Marina and Surf Shack at the Margarita Resort, at 0 Duval Street next to the Ocean Key Resort, the Galleon Marina, Marriott Beachside, and at the Hyatt Centric Resort. **Sunset Watersports** (305) 296-2554 leaves from Key West Bight, Smathers Beach, Parrot Key Resort, and Hurricane Hole Marina. **Barefoot Billy's** (305) 900-3088 services both the Casa Marina Resort and the Reach Resort. Or just Google 'jet ski Key West' and research which tour sounds best for you.

Type: Activity Cost: $100 to $140 for up to a two-hour tour, or $100/hour free range When: Year 'round

Jet Ski

Paint

Type: Activity Cost: Depends on class and supplies When: Year 'round Phone: TSKW, 533 Eaton Street (305) 296-0458, and Honest Works Island Pottery, 1203 Duval Street (419) 308-9221

Whether you bring your supplies with you or scrounge up an easel, paints and palette here, Key West is an inspiration of creativity for thousands. The Studios of Key West (TSKW) offers classes and workshops, serving over a thousand people each season, with more than fifty classes in a range of media for artists from beginners to professionals. Their instructors include year-round local artists, and artists visiting from across the globe. At their new facilities, TSKW presents exhibitions in two spaces for your enjoyment. Elsewhere, if you'd like to try your hand at making your own pottery, Honest Works Island Pottery offers pottery classes, as well as paint-your-own pottery for locals and tourists alike.

'Magic' Frank Everhart has been delighting audiences with his special brand of comedy, antics and up-close magic at the Schooner Wharf Bar for over sixteen years. Frank's bar magic is highly interactive with his own personal touch that makes you feel welcome and part of the show. For those fortunate enough to get a front row seat, hang on tight to your cocktail and prepare for adventure. Open nightly at 9pm Wednesday through Sunday night. Pull up a stool at Frank's Magic Bar. Its an opportunity to leave this world for a while and get lost in a sea of incredible island magic.

Type: Magic
Cost: Free, plus tips
When: Year 'round
Phone: (305) 292-3302

70 *Frank's* Magic Bar

Located at Schooner Wharf Bar

Get Your Dance On!

Although there's no reason whatsoever you can't dance at every bar in town if you get the itch, there is only one place with a dance floor the size of the entire club, and that's upstairs at Rick's in the Rick's/Durty Harry's Entertainment Complex. The best DJs, laser lighting, disco ball, smoke machines, and easy access bars in every direction.

Type: Activity Cost: Generally no cover When: Year/round, seven nights a week Phone: (305) 296-5513

Located at 202 Duval Street

Fringe Theater (305) 731-0581
fringetheater.org

credit | Roberta DePiero

THE PRODUCERS

A MEL BROOKS musical

Key West Theater
512 Eaton Street
(305) 985-0433
thekeywestthe-
ater.com

Waterfront Playhouse 310 Wall Street
(305) 294-5015 waterfrontplayhouse.org

WATERFRONT PLAYHOUSE

DIRTY ROTTEN SCOUNDRELS

Tennessee Williams Theater 5901 College Road
(305) 295-7676 twstages.com

68

Type: Theater
Cost: Tickets vary
When: Year 'round,
but season usually
lasts winter thru
spring

See a Show

Red Barn Theatre 319 Duval Street
(rear) (305) 296-9911 redbarnthe-
atre.com

67

Blue Hole

Type: Nature Cost: Free
When: Year 'round

Visit the Blue Hole on Big Pine Key, at MM 30. At the stoplight make a left onto Key Deer Blvd. and the Blue Hole will be on your left. Part of the National Key Deer Refuge, this is an abandoned limestone quarry used for nearby road fills and Henry Flagler's Overseas Railroad that has filled with rainwater (on the top) and heavier saltwater (below) that seeps in from the limestone. Fish, turtles, birds, snakes, invasive green iguanas, and American alligators can be found here. You may also see a few Key Deer running around.

Located at 175 Key Deer Blvd., Big Pine Key

Be Courteous
and Considerate

If this offends, sorry, that's not the intention, but a reminder never hurts... Sometimes the excitement of vacations are overwhelming, but a lot of us live here. Some tips: Streets aren't sidewalks. But sidewalks are! Please don't leave your garbage and unfinished drinks on walls and porches. There are garbage cans everywhere. When you're looking for a spot to park and there are several other people behind you, there's no need to stop in the middle of the road and evaluate each spot you're passing. Pull over anywhere and let everyone by. We've got to get to the bar and start making drinks! When you're on a bike, use common sense. If you're not going the speed limit, please ride on the side so others may pass. On Roosevelt, and other tight, major roads, it's smarter to use the sidewalk (not on Duval Street). There are lots of bike lanes (and they only go one way -- thanks!) When on foot, remember there are others sharing the sidewalk. There's no need to make people coming from the other direction play Red Rover. Whether there's ten or two of you, you can go single file for a few seconds, rather than make them step out into the street to get around. There's no reason to yell or honk your horns, especially at night. Look twice for scooters and try to recycle whenever possible. Lastly: please don't urinate in our yards. Only saying this because once a week or so I have to stop someone who has come inside my gate while in-between barhopping, or heading to their hotel, to pee. There are bathrooms everywhere! Slow down. We're not the mainland! Be kind. Be courteous. Say hi! We're one human family in Key West. Thanks! PS. Of course, none of these recommendations are for YOU, they're for that other guy.

Type: Advice
Cost: All advice is free
When: Always

66

65
The Driftwood Castle

Type: Adventure
Cost: Exploring is always free
When: Year 'round

Past where Boca Chica Road ends, Geiger Key

If you turn on Boca Chica Road at the Circle K on Big Coppitt Key (mile marker 10.5) and just keep going to the end, eventually you'll reach a barricade which blocks car travel, with the secluded and elusive Geiger Key Beach on one side (popular with runners, rollerbladers and stroller walkers) and the Naval Air Station on your right. Beyond that point the pavement has been washed away entirely, irreparably damaged years ago by Hurricane Wilma, and never repaired. Alongside the barricade stands an ominous (or exciting, depending on your outlook) sign: "Clothing optional beyond this point," there to protect any unsuspecting travelers. If you have children or you're offended by nudity, it's best to heed the sign's warning. After the initial stretch of sand and pavement you'll reach the flip flop memorial – a portion of chain link fence adorned with discarded shoes. Continue on and you'll finally reach an elaborate and mysterious beautiful structure of driftwood, coral and found objects that resembles a fairytale castle – with multiple rooms and levels that have tables and beach chairs - built by mysterious hermits, the homeless, trolls or mermaids, depending on who you talk to.

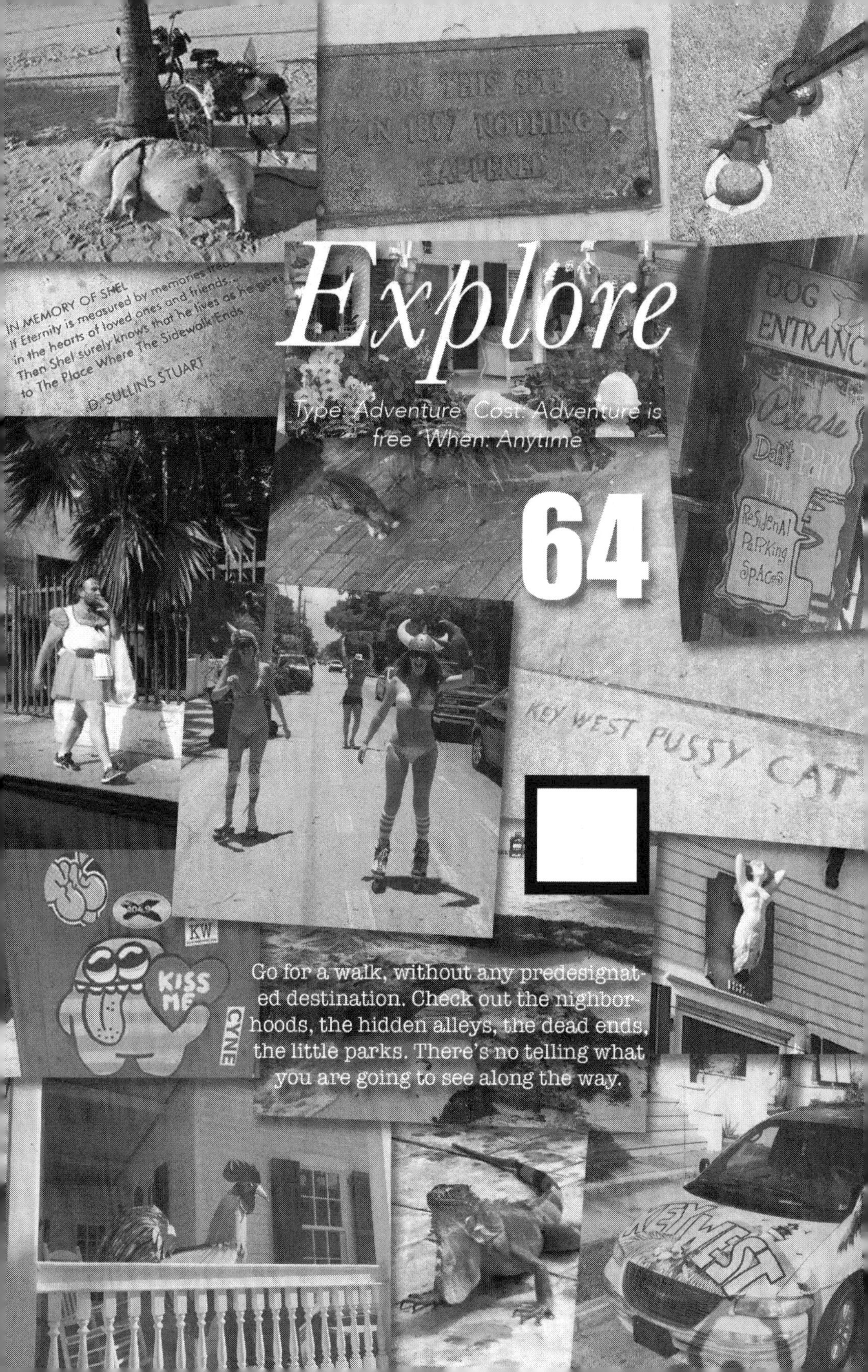

Explore

Type: Adventure Cost: Adventure is free When: Anytime

64

Go for a walk, without any predesignated destination. Check out the nighborhoods, the hidden alleys, the dead ends, the little parks. There's no telling what you are going to see along the way.

IN MEMORY OF SHEL
If Eternity is measured by memories from in the hearts of loved ones and friends...
Then Shel surely knows that he lives as he goes to The Place Where The Sidewalk Ends
D. SULLINS STUART

ON THIS SITE IN 1897 NOTHING HAPPENED

DOG ENTRANCE

Please Don't Park Thru Residential Parking Spaces

KEY WEST PUSSY CAT

KISS ME

KEY WEST

63

Type: Zoo Cost: Free of charge,
donations accepted When:
Second and fourth Sundays of
each month 1:00 - 3:00pm
Phone: 305-293-7300

The Animal Farm opened in 1994
in an open area underneath the
Monroe County jail facility. Home
to over 250 animals, they provide
a haven for animals which have
been abandoned, abused, confis-
cated or donated. Families may
come to visit horses, a steer, pigs,
goats, sheep, bunnies, alligators,
tropical birds, kinkajous, sloths, a
lemur, Kramer the emu, a family
of Patagonian cavys, tortoises
and turtles, snakes and many
more. County inmates care for
animals in the hopes they will
carry that lesson on in their lives
once they are released from jail.

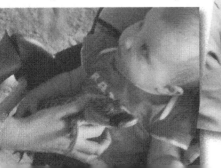

BUCKY

5501 College Rd on Stock Island

Spring Break

Type: Advice When: Whenever the colleges let out, usually in March

62

Great if you're a spring breaker. If you're not, you may want to avoid the first few weeks of March. You'll hear them, herds of college students riding down the streets on scooters, all honking their horns to let everyone know how free they are and how much fun they're having. There's a lot of noise, sex in alleys, puking, fighting, kids passed out in bars and front yards, all on Daddy's credit card. Bartenders and servers generally work for little to no tips for a couple of weeks, or wait on ten-tops where everyone has waters and a salad and wants to split the check ten ways, then get angry when it takes five minutes to separate the checks. But it is what it is. A right of passage. Because everyone who works down here was also once a spring breaker. Oh, and wait till you see what the beaches look .like in the mornings.

Type: Attraction
Cost: $22 adults, children 4-12 $11, under 4
free When: Year 'round Phone: (305) 743-2552

The Turtle Hospital

The Turtle Hospital is a fully functioning veterinary hospital for sick and in-
jured sea turtles that rescues, rehabili-
tates, and releases them back in the
Florida Keys. Guests are invited to take
a guided educational tour of the hospital
facilities and the sea turtle rehabilitation area. This educational experience
lasts approximately 90 minutes and
provides a presentation on sea turtles
as well as a behind the scenes look at
the hospital facilities and rehabilitation
area. At the end of each program guests
are invited to feed the permanent residents. Educational programs run hourly
from 9am to 4pm, and the Education
Center and Gift Shop is open daily from
9am – 6 pm. Reservations are highly
recommended.

2396 Overseas Highway, Marathon, MM 48.5

Strip Clubs

Whereas some gentlemen's clubs in town open and close depending on whatever lawsuits they're entangled in, you can always get scrubbed, teased, grinded on, and taken advantage of any night of the week in Key West if your libido is in charge of your wallet (or purse). The most beautiful women from around the world are here to take care of your most primal fantasies and needs, whether you're a man or a woman, or both, or here together. I had so many great photos for this page, but I can't seem to find them. Check out: **Red Garter** 208 Duval Street (305) 296-4964 2pm to 4am
Bare Assets 1029 Truman Avenue (305) 296-3979 4pm to 4am
Teasers 218 Duval Street (305) 292-0486 3pm to 4am

60

Located just an eight minute boat ride from Key West on the secluded island of Sunset Key, Latitudes boasts breathtaking views of the Gulf of Mexico, shady palm trees and tiki torches illuminating the night sky. You'll dine on exquisite island cuisine served indoors or alfresco in the most romantic setting you can possibly imagine, with an exquisite view of the sunset. Advance reservations are required. (Your reservation time is actually your boat departure time on one of their private boats.) Parking is complimentary in the Margaritaville Resort parking garage. Bring your ticket to the restaurant for validation. Serving breakfast, lunch and dinner. Contemporary American, Seafood, Caribbean.

59

Latitudes

Type: Restaurant Cost: Fine dining
When: Year 'round Phone: (305) 292-5394

Slip 29 in the Margaritaville Resort Marina, 245 Front Street

58 *Kayak*

On the northeast end of Key West is a protected back-country mangrove forest that is still relatively unspoiled by development where you can get up close and personal with unique coral, colorful sponges, queen conch, star-

Lazy Dog Adventures 5114 Overseas Hwy (305) 295-9898 lazydog.com $40/person 2 Hour Guided Tour, $60/person 4 Hour Guided Kayak/Snorkel Tour, Explore on your own: $25 for 1/2 Day, $40 for Full Day

fish, jellyfish, sea cucumbers, crabs, anemones, urchins, and tropical fish from aboard a one-seat or two-seat kayak. Explore fantastic tidal creeks, meander through islands of exotic red mangroves or "walking trees," which grow in salt

Clear Kayak Tours 231 Margaret Street excursionsofkeywest.com $99/person 3 hours 813-321-9702

The only 100% clear kayaks in Key West. You will also be able to cool off and snorkel as our tour is located very close to a shallow wreck site.

Kayak Kings of Key West Cow Key Marina, 5001 5th Ave, Key West, FL 33040 (305) 896-9006 kayakkingskeywest.com $45/person 2 hours, $55/person 3 hour private tour

water. Mangroves grow into magnificent forests with tangled roots that form natural winding paths that can easily be kayaked through. The roots of these unique forests are the nursery ground for many of our reef fish and invertebrates

Boca Chica Marine Life Kayak Tour at Blue Planet Kayak Eco-Tours (305) 809-8110 blue-planet-kayak.com $50/2.5 hours. Sheltered from the wind, there are no waves. It's an ideal trip for beginners and pros alike.

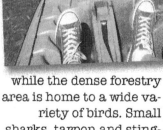

while the dense forestry area is home to a wide variety of birds. Small sharks, tarpon and stingrays are commonly spotted, as is the spectacular spotted eagle ray. Bring a waterproof camera.

Kayak Rentals at Most Oceanside Hotels and Beaches, too

57 ☐

Sexy
Bull
Riding

Type: Attraction/Activity
Cost: No cover When: Year
'round Phone: (305) 735-4292

Cowboy Bill's has the country music market cornered in Key West with the best live country bands that have ever plugged in their guitars. Conveniently located in the middle of the newly renovated historical district at 618 Duval Street. Enjoy dining, sports, pool tables, girls spinning on poles, live country music, and dancing every night, plus Salsa Loca Mexican food, and $2 PBRs all day, every day. Sexy Bull Riding Contest every Wednesday night with prizes up to $1000. And no, the clothes don't always stay on. Yee haw!

Located at 618 Duval Street

56

South Florida
Symphony Orchestra

The South Florida Symphony Orchestra (Boca Raton, Ft.Lauderdale, Key West, Miami) is the manifest dream of Music Director and Conductor Sebrina Maria Alfonso. Not an easy undertaking in an island community located at the end of a sparsely populated, one hundred and fifty-mile long, rural chain of islands. Maestra Alfonso, the first Cuban/American conductor invited to conduct Cuba's premier orchestra, was born and raised in Key West, a sixth-generation Conch. Even

with clear success and accolades throughout the years as she studied and performed across the country and in Europe, Ms. Alfonso returned to Key West and founded the Key West Symphony Orchestra in August 1997, recruiting forty-eight musicians from symphonies around the country. Upcoming performances might include a Broadway homage to Tony Award-winning musicals, Mendelssohn overtures, Bach concertos, Tchaikovsky symphonies, and/or a Rachmaninoff piano concerto.

Type: Concert Cost $25 to $85 When: Throughout the year, check sflso.org for schedule Phone: 305-295-7676

Florida Keys Community College, 5901 College Rd.

Dress Down

Ladies, unless you're here for a wedding or a funeral, leave your heels, nightclub dresses and most of your make-up at home. There's no need for them here, and chances are, you'll stick out like a sore thumb. This is flip-flop and bikini territory, where there are few to no dress codes (shirts and shoes required in fine dining restaurants, but that means flip-flops and tees), and the heat, humidity and water makes make-up pretty much pointless. Guys, no ties or jackets, ever. Leave your long pants and long sleeves at home, too. You won't need them. In those rare cases in the dead of winter when it might dip down into the 60's (and rarely the 50's), just pick yourself up a long-sleeved Key West souvenir hoodie or tee. If you require getting all dolled up before you can even consider hitting the nightlife, you've probably come too far south. The crowded streets of South Beach, with their $15 cover charges and $24 drinks, might be a little bit more up your alley. In Key West, we're WAY laid back .

Type: Advice Cost: Free

54 □

Firehouse Museum

Built in 1907, this is one of the oldest fire stations in the state of Florida. History buffs can learn much about the colorful southernmost island through its firefighting heritage. The museum is housed at the former Fire Station No. 3, which was active from 1907 until 1998. When the station first opened, the Key West Fire Department consisted of twelve paid men and 200 volunteers with horse drawn steamers and hose carriages. The station has endured several hurricanes. On display in the engine bay is their 1929 American La France pumper and a number of other artifacts dating from the early 1900s.

Type: Museum
Cost: $10, kids
under 12 free,
locals and fire-
fighter discount
When: Year
'round
Phone: (305)
849-0678

1025 Grinnell Street

Key West Historic Memorial
Sculpture Garden

53

Type: Attraction
Cost: Free
When: Year 'round

The Key West Historic Memorial Sculpture Garden features 36 magnificently cast bronze busts of the men and women who have had some of the greatest impact on Key West, created by master sculptor James Mastin. A bronze plaque on each pedestal tells not only the history of the selected person but also reveals a fascinating part of the island's history. Busts include Ernest Hemingway, Henry M. Flagler, William Curry, Sandy Cornish, John Geiger, Sister Louis Gabriel, Eduardo Gato, Ellen Russell Mallory, John Watson Simonton, Asa Forseyth Tift, Harry S. Truman, and William Whitehead, among others. Alongside, Mastin's magnificent sculpture "The Wreckers," at 18 feet long and 25 feet high, captures the spirit of Key West as a bold, boisterous, and bustling sea town out on the frontier of young America, depicting Key Westers saving lives and cargo from a vessel come to ultimate peril on our reef. You can have your name engraved upon a walkway brick for $60 per name/per brick. Details at KeyWestSculptureGarden.org. or contact Hope Casas at (305) 294-4142.

Ernest Hemingway
1899–1961

Born in Oak Park, IL in 1899. During World War I, volunteer in the Red Cross Ambulance Corps, at which After the war, he settled in Paris where he w 1926, Hemingway published his firs tional acclaim. Returning to ey West on o lea a new y out it was no o learn the city. Finding the atmosphere to visit again and finished

Located in front of the Waterfront Playhouse, adjacent to the Key West Chamber of Commerce in Mallory Square

52 *Street Vendors*

Buy something unique from a street vendor. Jewelry, a book, a piece of art, a hat or basket woven from palm leaves. Have your portrait done or get a caricature made. Put a parrot or boa constrictor on your shoulder for a photo op. It may look as though they just rambled in and set up a makeshift shop, but there is a lot of licensing hoops to jump through and tax rigamorole that must be dealt with before these vendors hit the streets. Feel free to haggle a little bit, and help keep capitalism flourishing, before someone outlaws these creative outcasts.

Type: Shopping Cost: Not much When: Year 'round

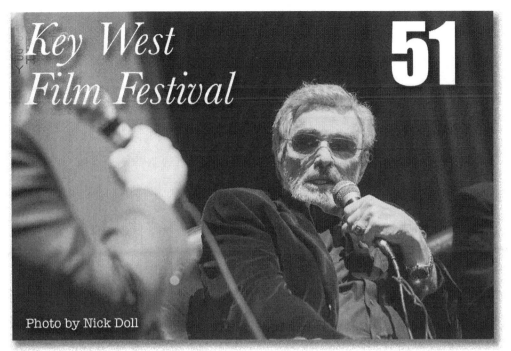

Key West Film Festival

Photo by Nick Doll

The Key West Film Festival is an annual celebration of film and filmmakers, showcasing films that represent a broad cross-section of categories that offer a broad set of opportunities for filmmakers, both aspiring and established, to show off what they've got. Whether you join in as a showcasing filmmaker, an audience member, a volunteer, or a partner, you can expect 30+ movie screenings at amazing screening venues such as historic theaters or outdoors on the beach, receptions at treasured Key West venues, interactive panel discussions, film critics movie selections, Q&A with directors, actors, producers and critics, movies before they hit theaters, planty of of live music, and Hollywood's finest discuss their latest projects or accept awards for their achievements.

Type: Event Cost: From sponsorship to attending events, the cost varies. For 2017 events and up-dated information for 2017, go to KWFilm-Fest.com When: Mid November Phone: (877) 722-2829

Photo by Rob O'Neal

Key West Outdoor Movies at Bayview Park

50

The Bayview Park Movie Series gives the local community (and tourists) the opportunity to watch a popular movie in a safe, community-based environment underneath the stars. This event is free to the public, is alcohol and tobacco free, and provides entertainment for all ages, including well-behaved pets. Starts at dusk. Rain dates scheduled the following Sunday, if possible. Movies have included Pete's Dragon, Moana, Napoleon Dynamite, Grease, and The Secret Life of Pets.

Type: Entertainment Cost: Free When: the 1st and 3rd Friday of every month, starting October through May. Phone: (305) 791-4375
scott@visualize-entertainment.com

Located at Truman Avenue and Jose Marti Drive

Conch Honk

49

Type: Event Cost: Free When: Early March, contact oirf.org
Phone: (305) 294-9501

Photos by Rob O'Neal

Aspiring "musicians" can test their skill on the conch shell (pronounced 'konk') at the annual Conch Shell Blowing Contest in the garden of the Oldest House Museum, free to enter and watch. Those lacking "instruments" can purchase conch shells on site. Trophies are awarded in four categories, with judging based on the quality, duration, loudness and novelty of the sounds produced. Key West's connection with the hardy sea mollusk goes far beyond instrumental uses of its fluted pink-lined shell. Native-born residents refer to themselves as conchs, and if you've lived in Key West for a seven-year duration you're formally allowed to call yourself a 'freshwater conch'. Uniquely painted and decorated cars, scooters and bikes are affectionately referred to as conch cruisers. The high school team is called the Conchs. Conch chowder and conch fritters are traditional island dishes, and the two-story wooden gingerbread houses in the historic Old Town district are called conch houses. In 1982 the Florida Keys and Key West proclaimed themselves the Conch Republic, and the shell remains an enduring symbol of the island chain.

Located at 322 Duval Street

48

Tropical Forest and Botanical Garden

The Key West Tropical Forest & Botanical Garden, filled with butterflies, birds, plants and beautiful flowers, is the only "frost-free" botanical garden in the continental United States, and home to many endangered and threatened flora and fauna. The forest has two of the last remaining fresh water ponds in the Keys and is a major migratory stopping point for neo-tropical birds from places as far as South America, as well as being home to many rare birds in the Florida Keys. Your visit begins with a smiling volunteer greeter at the education center. After a short film, browse the photo walls, then pick up a Garden Guide that describes the eight self-guided tours, two wetland habitats and two butterfly gardens. The lush courtyard has a waterfall wall of tropical plants and playful turtles. Meander through a one acre butterfly habitat with over 23 species discovered and stroll through a lush canopy of tropical palms and trees. Discover the hidden pond and maybe get lucky enough to see a rare resident white crowned pigeon or bald eagle!

Type: Attraction Cost: Adults $7, seniors $5, kids under 12 free When: Daily 10 - 4pm, except holidays. Contact kwbgs.org Phone (305) 296-1504

Located at 5210 College Rd

The Headdress Ball

Going on for thirty-five years now, the Headdress Ball, an official event of Fantasy Fest, is a major fundraiser for the Key West Business Guild, the nation's oldest LGBT Chamber of Commerce. Over the years the Ball has been staged in some of the island's favorite bars, from the The Monster, to The Copa, to Epoch, and even under a tent at the infamous Atlantic Shores Resort. Prizes over $5000 in cash! It's a grand evening of high performance and not a lot of rules! This is an adult-themed, all welcome event. In Key West, there's only one reason for a closet and that's to hold costumes! Emceed by the one-and-only Tom Luna.

Photos by Larry Blackburn

Type: Event Cost: Always sells out - keystix.com
When: Last week of October Phone: 305-294-4603
Info: Facebook.com/head-dressballkeywest

Play a Round or Two

The Key West Golf Club is the only Caribbean golf course in the United States. Golf legend Rees Jones masterfully designed the Key West Golf Course, an 18 hole, 6,500 yard course spread over 200 acres of beautiful Florida Keys foliage and wildlife to be a challenge to players of all abilities. Come meet all the exciting challenges of the Key West Golf Course, including the infamous "Mangrove Hole" (143 yards, par 3 that is played completely over a

field of thickly intertwined tropical mangroves). Lessons are also available.

Type: Activity Cost for 18 holes: Summer rates $75, winter rates $99. Twilight (after 1:00) summer rates $55, winter rates $75. Other discounts may be found online, as well as rates for club rental, bag storage, locker rental and buckets of balls for driving range. When: Year 'round Contact: (305) 294-5232 for tee time reservations, or check KeyWestGolf.com.

Located at 6450 E. College Road, Stock Island

West *Martello*

A tropical garden set in the ruins of an old Civil War fort, right on the ocean, with winding paths, blooming orchids and bromeliads, a water lily pond, waterfall, and a beautiful and popular venue for weddings and other events. This historic tower was built in 1862 and is one of three remaining Civil War era structures on the island. Although it was often used for target practice by the United States Navy, the fort was never actually involved in a battle. It is now home to the Key West Garden Club, a non-profit organization run by volunteers, and one of the island's last remaining free tourist attractions. In early March. the public is encouraged to enter their blooming orchids for possible awards in the Key West Orchid Society Show, held over two consecutive days. Orchid sales and supplies, awarded orchids displays, raffle items, art, food and more is offered. Free admission and parking.

Type: Garden Cost: Free When: 9:30 to 5:00 seven days a week (except holidays) year 'round Contact: Key West Garden Club (305) 294-3210, Key West Orchid Society (305) 509-7744 KeyWestOrchidSociety.org

1100 Atlantic Blvd. at Higgs Beach

B.O.'s Fishwagon

44

Type: Restaurant Cost: Moderate
When: Year 'round
Phone: (305) 294-9272

If ever there was a don't-miss eatery that typified the crazy, laid-back aura of Key West, it's B.O.'s Fishwagon, an open-air mangrove shack a block inland from the Harbor Walk that looks as if it were constructed with debris by a hurricane carpenter. Buddy Owen started his operation more than 25 years ago (that's from the web site where most things are dated 2014) but for the perfect fish sandwich and great live music on Friday nights, this is the coolest place you'll visit in Key West. Soft-shelled crab, fried cracked conch, fried fish platters, beer and wine...and there is so much to look at. Hours vary upon hangovers and how good the fishin' is going.

Corner of William and Caroline Streets

43

Bahai Honda
State Park

Type: Activity Cost: $8 per vehicle, $2 pedestrians and bicyclists, $4 motorcycle When: 8:00 a.m. til sunset, year 'round Phone: 305-872-3210, info@bahia-hondapark.com

Featuring an award winning beach and historic bridge, Bahia Honda State Park at mile marker 37 in the Florida Keys has become a favorite destination for visitors to our island paradise. The park, encompassing over 500 acres and an offshore island offers some of the best snorkeling and beachcombing in Florida. The perfect and quiet getaway for the entire family. The concession service provider offers a complete gift shop, snack bar, kayak rentals and daily snorkeling tours to the fabulous Looe Key National Marine Sanctuary. Daily departures are 9:30am, 1:30pm and/or 4:45pm daily. Each trip provides 1.5 hours of snorkeling, plenty of time to explore this fabulous coral reef. Free 24 hour WiFi at concession building. Bahia Honda State Park has many shore activities for the land lover: camping, lodging, bicycling, fishing, and many park programs.

Located at 36850 Overseas Highway (MM 37)

□

Swim with a Dolphin

The Dolphin Research Center is a dolphinarium on Grassy Key near Marathon. The 90,000-square-foot series of saltwater lagoons carved out of the shoreline is home to a family of dolphins and California sea lions, along with a lot of cats, exotic birds, and the occasional iguana. It features experiences where visitors can learn about marine mammals and the environment, and also swim with, hand-signal, or enjoy other interactive programs with the dolphins. It opened in 1958 as Santini's Porpoise School, and some of the early dolphins, including Mitzi, Little Bit and Mr. Gipper, starred in the Flipper movie. Through education, research and rescue, Dolphin Research Center promotes peaceful coexistence, cooperation and communication between marine mammals, humans and the environment we share with the well being of DRC's animals taking precedence. The facility is open daily to the public with informative narrated behavior sessions and educational presentations offered throughout the day. There are also a number of interactive programs available. Dolphin Camp, Teen DolphinLab classes, and Adult DolphinLab courses offer week-long educational opportunities for various age groups.

All of the adult courses are college-accredited. There are also a variety of other one-day and overnight educational programs available for school and youth groups such as Dolphin Day Trips, Dolphin Discovery and Dolphins: Dusk to Dawn. *Type: Activity Cost: General admission: adults: $28, military/veterans $25, children 4-12: $23, children 3 and under free. Dolphin Encounter $199 ea. Family Dolphin Splash $139 ea. Ultimate Trainer for the Day $695. VIP Experience $475. Researcher Experience $475. Play with the Dolphin $85. Meet the Dolphin $50 per program participant. Dolphin Explorer $75. Paint with a Dolphin $65. When: Open 7 days a week, 9 a.m. to 4.30pm, year 'round Phone: Program reservations - 305-289-0002, Offices - 305-289-1121 Contact their website for program details and information: dolphins.org*

Located at 58901 Overseas Highway, Grassy Key

New Release!!

The Best of Key West Volume Three

The best musicians. The best singers. The best songwriters. All together on the bestselling CDs in Key West. It's like taking the experience of walking down Duval Street home with you. Order a CD or a digital download from iTunes or CDBaby.com. Just search for 'The Best of Key West', and they'll pop right up for you, to sample or to buy. $1 from the sale of each CD goes to benefit the Sister Season Fund of Key West.

A Bucky Montgomery Production ©2017

Sleep In

Slow down. Relax. Kick back. There's no need to set an alarm. Wake up when you wake up. Then turn over and go back to sleep again for a little-while. Everything will still be here waiting for you in an hour or two. Be like a local. Be a little bit late. It's irie. Nothing is better for peace of mind that giving your body the rest it deserves. And later on? Take a nice long nap. Chances are you'll be out late again tonight.

Type: Advice Cost: Nada
When: As often as possible

Anywhere You Wake Up

40

Hemingway Days

For the better part of eleven years (from 1928 through 1939) Ernest Hemingway wrote some of his most enduring works in his Whitehead Street studio, including A Farewell To Arms, Green Hills of Africa, To Have and Have Not, and For Whom the Bell Tolls, while spending his leisure hours fishing and socializing with local and literary cohorts. His zest for life, literary accomplishments and enduring affection for the island he called home throughout the 1930s are commemorated each July, during the annual Hemingway Days celebration. Events include a look-alike contest for stocky white-bearded men resembling Hemingway, a commemoration of the anniversary of Ernest's July 21 birth at Sloppy Joe's Bar, literary readings and book signings, an awards ceremony for the renowned short story literary competition, a theatrical premiere, a paddle board race, a 5K run, a museum exhibit of rare Hemingway memorabilia, a zany "Running of the Bulls" and a three-day marlin tournament recalling Hemingway's devotion to the deep-sea sport.

Type: Event Cost: Free to watch, free to compete When: Hovers around July 21 Phone: (305) 296-2388 Contact: sloppyjoes.com

Located at Sloppy Joe's Bar, 201 Duval Street

39

Derby Dames

Type: Events Cost: $5, free for kids under 12 When: One bout per month Phone: (407) 418-4171 keywestderbydames.com

The Key West Derby Dames are a women's flat track roller derby team comprised of women skaters of all age ranges and walks of life: nurses, mothers, social workers, artists, educators, scientists, and members of the military. The organization is run entirely by the skaters, with each skater contributing her own unique skills on and off the track. As the southernmost derby team in the U.S. they live all up and down the Keys, from Tavernier to Key West, and are always looking for new women and men to get involved in the league, as skaters, referees, or non-skating officials. Come watch monthly bouts at the Southernmost Hockey Rink on Bertha Street. Doors open at 6 pm, first whistle is at 6:30 pm. They practice on Sundays from 5:30 – 8:00 pm and Thursdays from 7:30 – 9:00 pm and 'fresh meat' practice is held Sundays from 3:30 – 5:15 pm.

Tim Campbell Images

Located on Bertha Street at Atlantic Blvd.

Flagler Station
HISTOREUM
38

Type: Museum Cost: Free (It says $3 but no one's ever there)
When: Year 'round Phone: (305) 293-8716 flaglerstation.net

The Flagler Station Over-Sea Railway Historeum will bring to life the history and legacy of Henry Flagler's Florida East Coast Railroad Key West Extension, once deemed 'the eighth wonder of the world'. In 1905, Flagler, 75 years old and one of the wealthiest men in the world (after partnering with John D. Rockefeller back in 1867 to form the Standard Oil Company) announced his plan to build a railway from Miami to Key West, 130 miles out to sea. He instructed his engineers, "Go to Key West." After eight years of combating mosquitoes, enduring three hurricanes, labor problems, the wilderness, hundreds of lives lost, and $30 million, on January 22, 1912 the first New York to Key West train arrived in the Southernmost City with Henry and his wife aboard. Enter now through the side of the Cuban Art Museum into a reconstruction of a section of the Key West Terminus. Inside you'll find a mercantile store filled with candies, turn of the century dolls and toys, dry goods, railroad memorabilia, gifts and related souvenirs. Watch film presentations and listen to storytellers tell tales of the men who made possible one of the greatest engineering and construction feats of the 20th century.

Located at 901 Caroline Street

Read a Book

If you didn't bring one with you, no problem. Stop by **Books and Books** at 533 Eaton Street, **Key West Island Bookstore** at 513 1/2 Fleming Street (our only two bookstores), or the public library at 700 Fleming Street. Read on the beach while you tan, or discover one of our hidden parks for some real peace and shade beneath the palms. Here's a list of a few of Key West's hidden jewels: **Bayview Park** (Truman Avenue & Jose Marti Dr), **Bill Butler Park** (Poorhouse Ln and Windsor), **Little Hamaca Park** (Government Rd), **MLK Community Pool** (300 Catherine St), **Nelson English Park** (300 Catherine St), **Indigenous Park** (1801 White St), and **Spottswood Park** (Seminole St and Alberta Ave).

Type: Relax Cost: Whatever your book costs
When: Every day if you can

37

36 *Mel Fisher Maritime Museum*

Despite suffering many personal losses during his sixteen year search for treasure (including the drowning death of his eldest son Dirk, his wife, and another diver) every day Mel Fisher optimistically told his crew, "Today's the Day". And on July 20, 1985, the $450 million dollar "Atocha Mother Lode" was finally found, over forty tons of silver and gold, including over 100,000 Spanish silver coins known as "Pieces of Eight", gold coins, Columbian emeralds, silver and gold artifacts and over 1000 silver bars. And that's only half of it... The rest of the treasure from the Nuestra Senora de Atocha and the Santa Margarita, the Spanish galleons that sank during a hurricane on September 6, 1622, near Key West, are still out there somewhere, waiting to be found, including 300 silver bars and 8 bronze cannons. Visit the Mel Fisher Maritime Museum for a glimpse of the 1622 fleet exhibit of the Spanish galleons, a thought provoking slave ship, and Key West African Cemetery exhibits which provide a stark look into the transatlantic slave trade and Key West's unique role in it. Learn about Spanish coins in the New World, the real pirates of the Caribbean, and the science of shipwrecks. If you're interested in taking some of the treasure home with you, it's for sale. A popular item you may see worn around town are Atocha coins dangling from necklaces, affectionately referred to on occasion as 'Key West dog tags'.

Type: Museum Cost: $15 adults, $12.50 students, $5 children When: Mon - Fri 8:30 to 5:00, Holidays and Weekends 9:30 to 5:00
Phone: (305) 294-2633 melfisher.org

Located at 200 Greene Street

Karaoke

From the awe-inspring to the downright terrible, there is apparently no end to the fad that never dies, karaoke, where, for better or worse, members of the audience become the star in the spotlight. And Key West embraces the tradition. Although karaoke hours are hard to pin down, there are five big venues, and countless smaller ones scattered about. Check out **Two Friends Patio Restaurant** on Front Street, **801 Bourbon Street** on Duval, **Aqua Nightclub** on Duval, **Rick's Downstairs** also on Duval, and the mother of all Key West karaoke bars, **Bobby's Monkey Bar** on Simonton Street, where, after the late night curtain calls of theater presentations and concerts, this is the karaoke destination of the cast members for many a late night after-party. *Type: Activity Cost: Singing is free When: Every night, 365 days a year*

35

34

Pigeon Key Art Festival

Pigeon Key is a small five-acre island located two miles west of Marathon. The Old Seven Mile Bridge, which connects the island to Marathon, is currently closed for repairs, due to reopen in May 2017. The only way to access Pigeon Key until then is via ferry boat which departs from the Visitor's Center, located at 1 Knights Key Boulevard at Mile Marker 47. Look for the Bright Red Train Car. Guided historical tours last about an hour. This allows you ample opportunity to explore the island, enjoy a picnic, snorkel, or fish off the dock.

Type: Activity Cost: $12, under 5 free When: 9:30am-4pm, year 'round Phone: (305) 743-5999

The Pigeon Key Art Festival, now in its 24th year, was moved to Marathon Community Park several years ago due to bridge and ramp repairs. It attracts exemplary artists and quality buyers from across the globe. More than seventy fine artists and craftsmen will be in attendance. Enjoy delicious local cuisine, live art, and an auction by preeminent celebrity marine life artist, Wyland. Enjoy

historical elements, entertainment, children's activities and educational programming. Your Art Festival admission entitles you to half price tickets on the daily ferry to Pigeon Key. *Type: Event Cost: $7 for both days, kids free When: February 3 and 4, 2018 Phone: (573) 680-5468 pkartfestival@gmail.com*

Located at Marathon Community Park, 200 Ocean, 36th St, MM49

Higgs Beach

Approximately 16.5 acres of ocean front vista offers a diverse array of activities and offerings. Within the Park, you'll find a Civil War Era Fort, Salute! on the Beach (a beachside café featuring a Caribbean take on Italian classics), the largest African Refugee Burial Ground in this hemisphere, one of the largest Aids Memorials in the country, swimming, snorkeling, sunbathing, beach volleyball, tennis, pickleball and a brand new beachside children's playground. Tropical Water Sports, a beach concessionaire, offers users a broad array of beach accessories for rent including beach chairs, umbrellas, kayaks, and paddleboards. Across the street is the city's largest dog park with separate runs for small and large dogs. There's also White Street Pier, and bocce ball across the street.

Type: Activities Cost: Beach is free, but there's plenty to splurge on for recreational and culinary purposes
When: Year 'round.

Located on the Atlantic Ocean at the end of White Street

Spoil Yourself

☐ **32**

Type: Advice Cost: Depends upon
the services When: Year 'round
Contact: Most hotels, and search
online. There are lots.

Key West may be a laid-back relaxation destination, but sometimes just getting here can wear you out. Airport delays, long car rides, checking in and getting settled, all can lead to tight necks and aching backs. Fortunately, Key West has plenty of spas that will soothe away your aches and pains and rejuvenate you from the inside out: massage, acupuncture, facials, pedicures, aromatherapies... Key West writer and local expert Claudia Miller describes ten of the best in this online article. She says, "Whether you're flying solo, on a romantic getaway, or a girl's weekend, these ten best spas in Key West will quickly put you on island time." Check it out here. Spoil yourself. You deserve it:
http://www.10best.com/destinations/florida/key-west/attractions/spas/

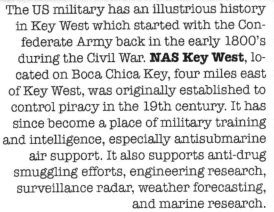

Salute a Soldier

The US military has an illustrious history in Key West which started with the Confederate Army back in the early 1800's during the Civil War. **NAS Key West**, located on Boca Chica Key, four miles east of Key West, was originally established to control piracy in the 19th century. It has since become a place of military training and intelligence, especially antisubmarine air support. It also supports anti-drug smuggling efforts, engineering research, surveillance radar, weather forecasting, and marine research.

Located on the Truman Waterfront on the western edge of Key West, the **USCGC Ingham** is one of only two preserved treasury-class United States Coast Guard cutters, and now a member of Key West Maritime Memorial Museum available for touring. She was the most decorated vessel in the Coast Guard fleet and was the only cutter to ever be awarded two Presidential Unit Citations.

Type: Museum Cost: $10, kids $5, under 6 free When: Tues - Sat 10-4, year 'round
Phone : (305) 292-5072

Located at Truman Waterfront at the end of Southard Street

Dine Out

30

Common tourist question: Where can I get good seafood? Answer: Everywhere. Seriously. Where to eat? Anywhere. Your decision only requires you to figure out whether you want to splurge for upscale fine-dining, or hit an economical fish shack. There are numerous restaurants on nearly every block of Duval, or just off Duval. And delightful neighborhood eateries built in century-old homes scattered all through Old Town. For top notch sushi, try **Ambrosia Japanese Restaurant** at 1401 Simonton. Delicious vegetarian can be found at **The Cafe** at 509 Southard. Key West's best barbecue at **Charlie Mac's** also on Southard at 404, next door to the famous Green Parrot Bar. One of local's favorite Italian joints is **La Trattoria** at 524 Duval Street. **Pepe's** at 806 Caroline has been around since 1909 and generally has a line at the door for their amazing breakfasts. There's the trendy **Kojin Noodle Bar** at 601 Southard #4. (Try a Can-O-Fun). There are numerous choices on the Harbor Walk. And for honest-to-goodness Cuban, you can't go wrong with **El Meson De Pepe** at Mallory Square, or the award-winning **El Siboney** at 900 Catherine Street. This is just a smattering of the fantastic cuisine choices available. If you're more into the nation-

wide chain restaurants (many have come and gone throughout the years - Hooters, TGI Fridays, Johnny Rockets, Planet Hollywood, Five Guys, and BurgerFi) we still have **Denny's**, **Hard Rock Cafe**, **Margaritaville**, **Outback Steakhouse**, **Benihana's**, and relative newcomer to Key West, **Señor Frogs**.
Type: Restaurant Cost: Varies

29

☐

Theater of the Sea

Type: Activity Cost: $34
adult, $23 child, under 2 free
When: Ticket counter 9:30
to 3:30, reservation office
9am to 10pm, year round
Phone: (305) 664-2431
theaterofthesea.com

SWIM TODAY!

Theater of The Sea
Marine Mammal Park
Islamorada, Florida

Twelve million gallons of ocean water are pumped in daily to supply water to the three-acre natural salt-water lagoons at Theater of the Sea in Islamorada. Get up close and personal with dolphin, sea lions, parrots, rays, sharks, lorikeets, sea turtles, and much more. General admission includes the dolphin, sea lion, and parrot shows, a bottomless boat ride, a lagoon-style beach, and a guided marine life tour with tropical fish, sharks, turtles, stingrays, alligators, and crocodiles. To go above and beyond general admission activities: Swim with a dolphin - $199. Wade with a dolphin - $185. Meet a dolphin - $95. Paint with a dolphin - $95. Ultimate private dolphin swim - $1755. Swim with the rays - $75. Meet the lorikeets - $45. Swim with the sharks - $95. Swim with a sea lion - $155. Meet a sea lion - $95. Paint with a sea lion - $85. Meet a sea turtle - $65. Sunset cruise - $70. Adventure and snorkel cruise - $115. All prices subject to change. There are discounts available which you can find by checking out their web site.

Located at 84721 Overseas Hwy (MM 84.5) Islamorada

Ripley's Believe It or Not Odditorium

You're greeted in the front lobby by a man-eating shark, an 8-foot tall statue of Capt. Jack Sparrow made from recycled car parts, and a beautiful carving of a landscape made entirely out of camel bone. More unbelievable exhibits await inside the 10,000 square foot historical building, a museum of the macabre, bizarre, and unusual, featuring 15 air-conditioned themed galleries with 550 exhibits and artifacts on two floors and outdoor balconies.

Type: Attraction Cost: $16.99 adults, $9.99 children ($4 online discount) When: 10am to 8pm, year 'round Phone: (305) 293-9939 keywest@ripleys.com

Located at 108 Duval Street

Key West Songwriters Festival

27 ☐

Five days, fifty+ shows, two hundred+ performers, the Key West Songwriters Festival is the largest festival of its kind in the world. Celebrating its 22nd year, the name is a bit misleading; there are more songwriters from Nashville and the rest of the country than there are Key West songwriters. Since 1997, BMI has been a presenting sponsor of the festival that has helped songwriters sell their songs, and musicians find fame. Shows start early afternoon and play into the late night, utilizing most of the island's clubs, restaurants, pools, and hotels, with a huge street party on Duval and Greene Streets on the weekend. *Type: Event Cost: Most of the shows are free. The shows that require advance ticket purchase go on sale in March and are usually sold out. When: Mid-May Contact: kwswf.com, keywestsongwritersfestival.com, or nashville@bmi.com*

26 □ *Go Green*

The Florida Keys Eco-Discovery Center features over 6,000 square feet of interactive exhibits including a mock-up of Aquarius, the world's only underwater ocean laboratory. Journey into the world of native plants and animals of the Keys, both on land and underwater, from the upland pinelands through the hardwood hammock, beach dune, mangrove shoreline, the seagrass flats, hardbottom, coral reef, and deep-shelf communities. Catch "Reflections of the Florida Keys," a short film on the diverse ecosystem of the Florida Keys. And be sure to check out the Mote Marine Laboratory Living Reef exhibit, a 2,500 gallon reef tank with living corals and tropical fish, a live Reef Cam, and other displays that highlight the coral reef environment.

Type: Environmental Cost: Free When: Year 'round, Tues. - Sat. 9am to 4pm. Contact: (305) 809-4750 FKEDC@noaa.gov.

Located at 33 E. Quay Road, at the end of Southard Street in the Truman Annex, across the street from Fort Zachary Taylor Historic State Park.

Reef Relief® is a nonprofit membership organization dedicated to improving and protecting our coral reef ecosystem. The center features a diorama of a healthy reef and a damaged coral reef that identifies commonly found coral species in the Caribbean, and conditions needed for healthy coral growth as well as ways the coral reef ecosystem may be harmed as a whole. A Google Earth© Oceans exhibit enables the viewer to visit coral reefs around the world. A theatre shows daily films related to coastal resource issues.

Type: Environmental Cost: Free, but donations appreciated When: Year 'round 10am – 4pm (Closed Sat. and Sun.) Contact: (305) 294-3100 reefrelief.org

Located at at 631 Greene Street, in the heavily trafficked Historic Seaport in Key West, next to the Conch Republic Seafood Company.

inside

Key West Kentucky Derby Party

Type: Event Cost: Millionaires Row (includes dinner and a reserved seat) around $50, the Infield around $10 When: First Saturday in May Phone: (305) 294-0555 aquakeywest.com

A complimentary mint julep. Good bourbon. Fancy hats and dresses for the ladies. Gawdy pastel plaid suits and bow ties for the gents. Hot browns. Derby pie. Red carpet. Horse racing on a giant screen and gambling all day! And all with a Key West island twist. "Millionaire's Row" gets you a reserved seat (or reserve a whole table with friends), a Kentucky hot brown open-faced turkey sandwich, a cup of burgoo with cornbread, a slice of Derby pie from Kern's Bakery in Louisville, and a real Mint Julep. "The Infield" gets you general admission and a real Mint Julep, no reservations necessary. Talk Derby to me! Horse races all day! Run, baby, run!

Located at Aqua Night Club, 711 Duval Street

24 Parades □

Key West sure loves a parade. There are a lot of them. And unlike many other parades around the country, many times guests from the sidelines are welcome to join in, or at least tag along behind. There are military parades on holidays such as Memorial and Veterans Day, the artistic Papio Kinetic Sculpture Parade, the Lighted Christmas Boat Parade on the Harbor (page 53), the Smallest Parade in the Universe, the City of Key West Christmas Parade, the KW Pet Masquerade (page 59), the Crooks Annual second Line, the Key West Dachshund Parade, the Key West Pride Parade Flag, Goombay Festival with the Junkanoo Band (page 23), the Zombie Bike Ride (page 34), the Local's Walking Parade, the Conch Republic Independence Celebration Parade (page 164), the Lighted Bicycle Parade, and then there's the granddaddy of them all, the Fantasy Fest Parade on the last Saturday of every October (page 188), the event that caps off two weeks of decadent partying.

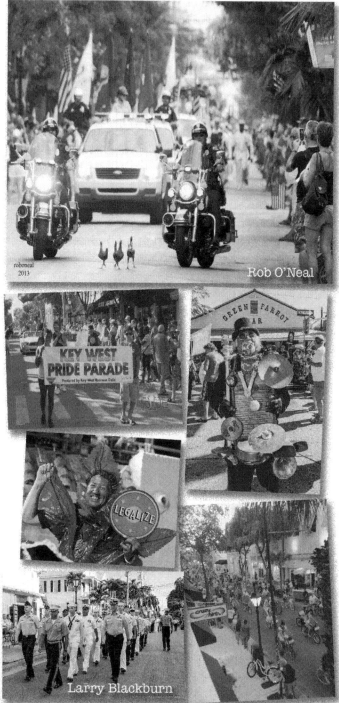

roboneal 2013

Rob O'Neal

Larry Blackburn

Freshwater Conch
GALA and CELEBRATION

23

Once you have lived in the Keys for seven consecutive years, you can celebrate with a night of fun, music, food, and drink, with friends, family, and even your dog. Come listen to amazing stories about how others arrived and why they stayed here, and take home an 'official' certificate proclaiming you a 'Freshwater Conch'. Dress is 'Key West formal'. Hosted by local celebrities. And if your dog has lived in Key West for a year, they'll consider that seven dog years, and certificates will be available for them as well. The Freshwater Conch Gala and Celebration is an official event of the Conch Republic Independence Celebration every April.

Type: Event Cost: Free to attend When: Mid April
Phone: (502) 322-7895 (text)

Located at Blue Macaw Island Eats and Bar

Recreation and
Friendly Competition

Pool tables: Waterfront Brewery, Bobby's Monkey Bar, Tattoos and Scars, Schooner Wharf, Cowboy Bill's, Hogfish Bar and Grill, Gas Monkey, Green Parrot. **Darts:** Don's Place, Shanna Key, Green Parrot, Whistle Bar. **Golden Tee/ Big Buck Hunter:** Schooner Wharf, Green Parrot, Island Dogs, Waterfront Brewery, Tattoos and Scars. **Tennis:** Island City Tennis 1310 Truman Ave, Paradise Tennis 1800 Atlantic Blvd, Bayview Park 1320 Truman Ave. **Volleyball:** Higgs Beach, Smathers Beach. **Basketball:** Bayview Park, Nelson English Park. **Skateboard:** Blake Fernandez Skate Park. **Bocce ball:** Turtle Kraals, Sonny McCoy Indigenous Park at White Street Pier.

Type: Activity Cost: Varies When: year 'round

21

Festivals

There are festivals, there are events, and there are festivals full of events, nearly every week, if not every day, in Key West, far too many to keep up with. Here are a few. For more info, they're easy to Google. Womanfest (September), Mystery Fest (June), Key Lime Pie Festival (4th of July weekend), Fantasy Fest (p. 188), KW Songwriters Festival (p. 149), Farmer's Market, Artisan's Market, Goombay Festival (p. 23), Lobsterfest (p. 8), KW Film Festival (p. 123), Florida Keys Seafood Festival (January), Key West Pride (June), Conch Republic Independence Celebration (p. 164), KW Food and Wine Festival (January), Brewfest (p. 47), Old Island Days Art Festival (February), Key West Holiday Fest (December), KW Africana Festival (June), MMITK Festival (June), Bubbafest (November), Guitar Festival (June), Key West to Cuba Festival (September), Pirates in Paradise Festival (December), Keystock Music Fest (March), Underwater Music Festival (July), Hemingway Days (p. 136), Winter Star Party (Feb-

ruary), Mel Fisher Days(July), WineDine Key West (Sept-Oct), Florida Keys Celtic Festival (January), and the ALR Coral Head Music Festival (February). *Type: Events/Activities/-Food Cost: Most are free When: Party never stops*

20

Type: Activity
Cost $60 to $90 When: Year Round

You basically have two choices for sunset/booze cruises, schooner or catamaran. **Fury's** popular **'Commotion on the Ocean'** features two hours on a 65-ft. catamaran, with live music, hot and cold appetizers, margaritas, champagne, beer, wine and sodas, $52 adult, $36 kids. For something a bit more upscale, try the all-inclusive **Key West Cocktail Cruise**, with craft beer, fine wine and craft cocktails aboard a spacious 47' catamaran, at $90/person. Departs from Garrison Bight on the M/V Good Times. If you want to sail like a pirate, check out the beautiful two-mast, 72' long **Appledore Star**, or the 105-foot, 1851 revival, **Schooner America 2.0**. Or maybe the 80-ft. 1800's-style schooner with the bright red pirate sails, the **Jolly Rover II**. All furnish complimentary champagne, wine, beer, and soft drinks. Passed hors d'oeurves are almost always provided. Around $75 to $95 per person. **Sebago Watersports** double-decker **Party Cat**, with a DJ, open bar, is just $59, kids $39 (under 5 free). The BEST way to book a cruise is to roam on down to the Harbor Walk between the Conch Republic Seafood Company and the Waterfront Brewery a couple of hours before sunset and see what's available.

19

Be Careful

This is the most important piece of advice in this book, because if you don't do this, you won't be able to do anything else. Be careful. Here's a few tips. Scooter accidents are the most common cause of major injuries on the island. There are several streets in Old Town that can zip you across the island because they have few lights and stop signs (Frances Street, Southard Street -one way west, and Fleming Street - one way east). But that doesn't stop cars from flying across your path, ignoring their stop signs. Watch for them. For some reason, there are abnormal vehicles that, for whatever reason, don't turn on their headlights at night. Watch for them, too. Don't hover your feet above the ground when riding your scooter. That's where the roadside flip-flop and the occasional toe come from. That's what the floorboard is for! After construction on N. Roosevelt was completed a few years back, they did two things which can be considered utterly ridiculous as far as safety standards go. One, it's legal to ride bikes on our most dangerous and fast-moving road. Even kids with training wheels. But DON'T. Cars zip from lane to lane, and there's a suicide lane in between the four lanes that already have a long list of injuries and fatlities. The wide sidewalks on either side offer a great view of the ocean, is wider than two car lanes, and generally have few to no pedestrians. Use common sense. Secondly, they added crosswalks, which seemed like a good idea at the time, but evidenced by multiple injuries and even deaths. It was not done correctly. Some pedestrians who feel they have right-of-way step right out into moving traffic, expecting four lanes of cars to see them and stop. Cars have yellow caution lights, but they never turn red, so even if three lanes stop, one may not. My advice is to wait until all four lanes are completely clear before crossing, which is what one should have been doing even before there were designated (and confusing) crosswalks. Better to be safe than sorry!

Type: Advice
Cost: Possibly your life. When: Always

18 Rent a Boat

Type: Adventure Cost:
From around $180 an hour
to $500 for eight hours
and everywhere in be-
tween When: Year 'round

Experience true freedom on the ocean in a skiff, center console, Boston whaler, deck boat, or even a pontoon boat with slides. There are multiple choices. You'll see boat rental signs everywhere when exploring the island. Perfect for chartered fishing trips, snorkel trips, reef trips for scuba divers, swimmers, anglers, sandbar trips, and romantic sunset getaways, from two to fourteen passengers. Your best bet is to go online and start exploring what's best for you. You'll find the prices comparable. **Key West Boat Rentals** (305) 791-1909 boatrentalsofkeywest, **Florida Keys Boat Rental** (305) 797-8954 boatrentalskw.com, **Boat Rentals Key West** (866) 545-1062 boatrentalskeywest.com, **Backcountry Boat Rentals** (720) 480-0557 backcountryboatrentals.biz

Cabaret
at La TeDa

17

You'll truly be wowed at The Cabaret at La Te Da, a Key West landmark for over thirty years. Talented singer/impersonators (there's no lip synching) transform into legendary stars like Marilyn Monroe, Lucille Ball, Bette Davis, Tina Turner, Barbra Streisand, Reba McEntire, and Judy Garland, right before your very eyes. The **Randy Roberts** Show is an all live tribute to some of the world's most loved performers. Randy's uncanny impersonations of Cher and Bette Midler have kept him in the spotlight for over twenty years. **Christopher Peterson** is a master of impersonations, and his comic timing is impeccable. The show is all live and audiences will be thrilled with his characterizations of Judy Garland, Liza Minnelli, and more. These classy performers know how to captivate an audience, get them involved, and keep them laughing until their faces ache. The stars usually leave Key West in the summer and return in the fall.

Type: Theater Cost: $26
When: Fall/Winter/Spring
Phone: (305) 296-6706 lateda.com

Located at 1125 Duval Street

Scuba Dive

16

Even if you've never been scuba diving before, you can do it in Key West in just one day. Already certified? Just hop aboard a boat and explore the third largest coral barrier reef in the world, the only living coral barrier reef in the United States. Approximately six miles offshore (about a 40 minute boat ride) there are an infinite number of locations for scuba and snorkeling in pristine water fifteen to thirty feet deep. There are 110 species of corals and over 500 species of

tropical fish in our coral reef community, all located within the National Marine Sanctuary. Your Captain chooses the actual reef location each day based on current conditions and with the goal of getting you to the best visibility and sea-state. Explore a sunken ship or experience a shallow night dive on the reef. For the more experienced, dive the Gen. Hoyt S. Vandenberg, rated the number one wreck in the world by the readers of Scuba Diving Magazine. She's the

second largest artificial reef in the world and a bucket-list dive for many experienced divers. Sunk in 2009, the Vandenberg measures ten stories high in the water column, the keel the deepest at 140 feet, located seven miles off the coast of Key West. If you've never experienced scuba diving but want to try it out, several locations offer a course to get you blowing bubbles in just one day. You begin in the morning with an instruction course to learn the basics of diving and how to use the gear (sometimes with a pool session), and then by the afternoon you're ready to go out on a reef trip to experience the underwater world with an instructor as your guide for your first two incredible dives. The reef is shallow and the PADI instructors are patient so you're always in good hands. Although this course does not certify you as a diver, it's a fun introduction to scuba diving. You're encouraged to research scuba diving options, but you can't go wrong with **Key West Dive Center** (866) 563-1805, **Dive Key West** (305) 296-3823, **Captain's Corner** (dive pool for beginner instruction) (305) 296-8865, or **Lost Reef Adventures** (305) 296-9737. *Type: Activity Cost: Generally between $135 to $195 When: Year 'round according to the weather*

15

☐

Photo by Rob O'Neal

Conch Republic
Independence Celebration

"We seceded where others failed". In 1982, the United States Border Patrol set up a roadblock and inspection point on US 1, in front of Skeeter's Last Chance Saloon, just south of Florida City. Vehicles were stopped and searched for narcotics and illegal immigrants. The Key West City Council complained repeatedly about the inconvenience for travelers to and from Key West, claiming that it hurt the Keys' important tourism industry. When the City Council's complaints went unanswered by the U.S. federal government and attempts to get an injunction against the roadblock failed in court, as a form of protest Mayor Dennis Wardlow and the Council declared Key West's independence. "Tomorrow at noon the Florida Keys will secede from the Union!" Wardlow announced to reporters gathered on the courthouse steps on his way out of the Miami District Court building. In the eyes of the Council, since the U.S. federal government had set up the equivalent of a border station as if they were a foreign nation, they figured they might as well become one. As many of the local citizens were referred to as Conchs, the nation took the name of the Conch Republic. As part of the protest, Mayor Wardlow was proclaimed Prime Minister of the Republic, and immediately declared 'war' against the U.S., symbolically breaking a loaf of stale Cuban bread over the head of a man dressed in a naval uniform. Citizens of the new republic began lobbing stale bread and conch fritters at federal agents, Navy sailors and Coast Guard personal in attendance. Approximately one minute after declaring 'war' on the United States, and firing a 'verbal shot' at the U.S., Wardlow surrendered to a nearby naval officer and requested $1 billion in foreign aid to compensate for "the long federal siege." The Conch Republic never received any foreign aid or war restitution, but the spectacle attracted enough publicity to convince the feds to remove the roadblock. We had won.

Each year in April the tongue-in-cheek activities continue and are celebrated over ten fun-filled days with multiple daily events, culminating in the Conch Republic Bloody Battle in the Key West Harbor, where the Conch Republic Navy and Air Force 'attack' and 'do battle' with our real Navy and Coast Guard ships with water hoses, water balloons, and volleys of stale Cuban bread and conch fritters, while spectators on shore and in boats watch the spectacle in relative safety. Here is a sample of the week's events: 'Conch Republic the Musical'; Kick-Off Party and Conch Shell Blowing Contest (p. 125); Earth Day Concert; Conch Republic Drag Race (p. 65); Royal Family Election; Conch Republic Secession Reenactment; Conch Cruise; March of the Sea Dogs Pet Stroll; Military Muster and Cocktail Party; Captains' Meeting for the Bloody Sea Battle; Hares n' Hounds Fun Run; Freshwater Conch Gala and Celebration (p. 154); Duval Street Mile; The 'World's Longest Parade', Awards Ceremony and After Party; Conch Fritter Eating Contest; the Great Battle Shoreside Viewing Party; the Naval Parade and Great Bloody Battle; Surrender Ceremony and Victory Party; Craft Show and Food Fest; Conch Crawl Bar Hop; Red Ribbon Bed Races (p. 84); the Pirate's Ball, Pig Roast, and Costume Competition; and the Diplomat's Brunch. "Long live the Conch Republic, and long live each and every one of you." -- Sir Peter Anderson

Type: Activities/Events When: Mid to late April Contact: conchrepublic.com

14

Key West Aquarium

Type: Attraction Cost: adults $15.03, children 4-12 $8.59, seniors $12.90. Discounts for online ticket purchase, seniors, military, locals, groups, and students. When: Open year 'round 9:00 to 6:00. Phone: (888) 544-5927 KeyWestAquarium.com

Mallory Square, Corner of Front St. and Whitehead St.

See the beautiful indigenous sea-creatures of Key West and the Florida Keys on 30 to 40-minute guided walking tours of the Key West Aquarium, established here back in 1934. Begin with a short introduction at the kid-friendly touch tank, followed with handfeeding of the stingrays, sharks and the Atlantic Shores exhibit. See sea turtles up close, octopus, barracuda, bonnethead sharks, tarpon, lionfish, jellyfish, grouper, and much more. During the tours, guests will have the opportunity to touch a live shark on the tail! Guided tours and shark feedings begin everyday at: 11:00am, 1:00pm, 3:00pm, and 4:30pm. Tickets are valid for two consecutive days.

Duval Crawl - Day

Measuring about one mile across, you can traverse the entire island from the Atlantic Ocean to the Gulf of Mexico and never be bored on Duval Street. The bars are open, singers are singing, restaurants are serving, but the word of the day is shopping. Browse the shops and galleries, drink from a coconut, and have some fresh seafood. Remember: you can't be drunk all day if you don't start in the morning.

13

Type: Shopping
When: Year 'round

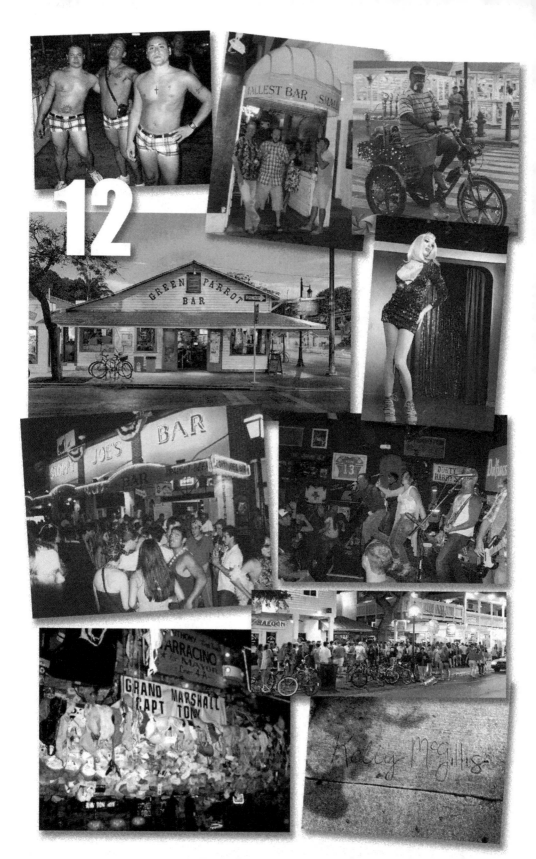

Duval Crawl - Night

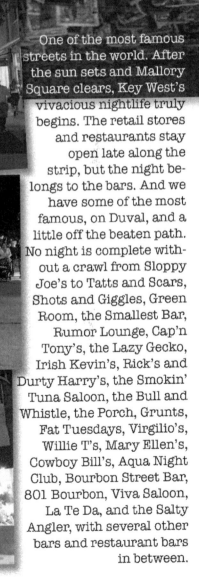

One of the most famous streets in the world. After the sun sets and Mallory Square clears, Key West's vivacious nightlife truly begins. The retail stores and restaurants stay open late along the strip, but the night belongs to the bars. And we have some of the most famous, on Duval, and a little off the beaten path. No night is complete without a crawl from Sloppy Joe's to Tatts and Scars, Shots and Giggles, Green Room, the Smallest Bar, Rumor Lounge, Cap'n Tony's, the Lazy Gecko, Irish Kevin's, Rick's and Durty Harry's, the Smokin' Tuna Saloon, the Bull and Whistle, the Porch, Grunts, Fat Tuesdays, Virgilio's, Willie T's, Mary Ellen's, Cowboy Bill's, Aqua Night Club, Bourbon Street Bar, 801 Bourbon, Viva Saloon, La Te Da, and the Salty Angler, with several other bars and restaurant bars in between.

11

Buy Local

Buy something made in Key West, local art, a local author's book, a trinket from a street vendor, or a unique Key West product from a unique Key West business, something found nowhere else in the world. Check out the Key West Cigar Factory, Kino's Sandals, the Waterfront Brewery, the Legal Rum Distillery, Key West Aloe, Peppers of Key West, Key West Winery, Baby's Coffee, Barb Grob's Local Luxe Jewelry, and Smilin' Bob's Smoked Fish Dip at our local grocery stores.

Type: Shopping Cost: Varies.

10 *Harbor Walk* ☐

The Harbor Walk has everything you came to Key West for. It curves around the Key West Harbor for about a half-mile from the Galleon Resort at one end to the Key West Express dock at the other. In between is a variety of ocean-themed delights: bars, shops, boats, restaurants, fish, and excursions of all kinds. It is the departure location of the sunset schooners and the booze cruises, jet skis, and fishing charters. You have classic bars like Turtle Kraals, Half Shell Raw Bar,

Located around the Historic Seaport

Type: Activity Cost: Free to walk, but bring money for everything else When: Year 'round

(continued from previous page) Conch Republic Seafood Company, and one of the 'can't miss' bars of Key West, the Schooner Wharf. There is live music, fine dining, bocce ball, and live turtle races. You have the shops of Lazy Lane, Kermit's Key Lime Pie Shoppe, the Waterfront Brewery, and A&B Lobster House. You can feed the tarpon, watch the pelicans dive, and if you're lucky, while the fishermen are cleaning the day's catch as they come into port, you might glimpse a nurse shark or huge grouper vying for scraps. The Harbor Walk is a favorite stopping point for curious manatee. You'll want to peruse Mac's Sea Garden, visit the Sea Turtle Museum or Reef Relief, have happy hour at the Boat House at the Commodore (local's favorite), buy some jewelry made from the coins of the sunken ship Atocha, and swim at Dante's Pool. This is where the millionaires park their yachts, and the Key Westers who make their homes on boats parked out to sea tie up their dinghies when they come to shore to go to work everyday. Make sure and check out the Wyland wall, first painted in September 1993, on the side of the newly renovated Waterfront Brewery at the end of William Street.

9 Dry Tortugas

Discovered by Ponce de Leon in 1513, the Dry Tortugas, named after the large population of sea turtles living in the surrounding waters, is made up of seven small islands. During the Civil War, historic Fort Jefferson was used as a prison. The fort's most famous prisoner, Dr. Samuel Mudd, was arrested for setting the broken leg of John Wilkes Booth after he assassinated Abraham Lincoln in 1865. He was later convicted and sentenced to life imprisonment here. Located just seventy miles from Key West, you can experience some of the best snorkeling in North America: majestic corals, many varieties of tropical fish, starfish, queen conchs and much more, easily viewed in shallow, pristine waters from five to fifteen feet deep. Complimentary fins, mask and snorkel are provided. Enjoy secluded beaches on day trips, or camp overnight (must bring your own water). For birders, these islands are a vital layover for migrating birds traveling between South America and the United States, making them a staple in the Great Florida Birding Trail. Nearly 300 species of birds may be found here.

Ticket Booth Located at 240 Margaret Street

Type: Attraction/Activity Cost: Day trip $175 adult, $125 child, $165 students, military, and seniors. Overnight camping $195 adult, $145 child, plus $15 - $30 park service camping fee When: Year 'round Phone: 305-985-1571 Reservations required

Yankee Freedom Ferry Terminal 100 Grinnell Street

Take a Tour by Trolley or Train

8

Type: Tour Cost: From $19
When: Year 'round, from
9:00/9:30am till 4:30pm

Old Town Trolley Tours (Thirteen stops - goes around the entire island.)

Cityview Trolley Tours (Nine stops in Old Town.) 105 Whitehead Street

(305) 294-0644

401 Wall Street
(855) 623-8289

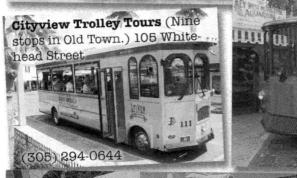

Conch Tour Train (Three stops.) Front and Duval Streets (888) 916-8687 (TOUR)

Hop Off and On Points All Over Town

180

Absolutely the first thing you must do when you come to Key West is take a tour on a Conch Tour Train or one of two trolleys. In 90 minutes or less you'll hit all the main points of interest, the beaches and the museums, while hearing stories of Key West's past, the flora and fauna, the architecture, and much, much more. Plus, you can hop off and on.

Drag Show

Somewhere over the rainbow-colored crosswalks, the 800 block of Duval Street soars as the hot spot for Key West's fun, raucous and outrageous drag shows, and everyone is invited. As the sun starts to set, you'll see the 'girls' out pushing the curbs in an effort to lure passersby into the shows, generally at 9pm and 11pm nightly, but there are often earlier shows. Reservations are suggested; day of show it's best to just show up early and get the best seat you can. There are two best bets. **801 Bourbon Bar** at the corner of Duval and Petronia Streets is ruled over by the Grande Dame of Drag herself, Sushi. (You've seen her for years on CNN in her world famous "Red High Heel Shoe" on New Year's Eve.) (305) 923-9296, 801bourbon.com. Or, at **Aqua Nightclub**, half a block away at 711 Duval Street where the Aquanettes spend part of the act amongst the audience to make the experience even more memorable. (305) 294-0555, aqua@aquakeywest.com. *Type: Entertainment Cost: $10 to $15 cover, but bring tip money When: The party never stops, year 'round*

Photo by Larry Blackburn

The 800 Block of Duval street

Live Music

Whether you like rock, blues, reggae, jazz, country, folk, or island sounds, some of the greatest musicians in the world perform on and off Duval Street in Key West.

6

Photos by Ralph de Palma

Type: Entertainment
Cost: Never a cover in
Key West
When: Year 'round,
from breakfast till
4:00am

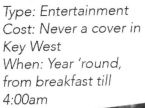

Fort Zack

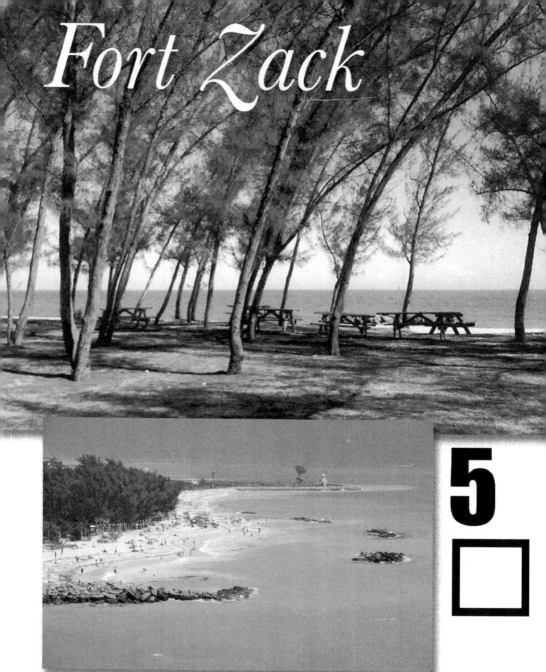

5

☐

The beach at Fort Zachary Taylor is the locals' beach. There are shade trees, picnic benches for parties and picnics, it's dog-friendly, and with three strategically-placed rock piles just a short walk or swim away (depending on low or high tide), novice snorkelers will get the greatest experience of their lives. These rocks are covered with colorful tropical fish. Swim, snorkel, tan, fish, lay on a raft. Visitors can also enjoy a short nature trail and bicycling within the park. The beachfront Cayo Hueso Café offers snacks, cold beverages (including beer and wine), beach sundries, and souvenirs. Completed in 1866, the now landlocked Fort Zachary Taylor played important roles in the Civil War and Spanish-American War. Guided tours of the fort are available daily.

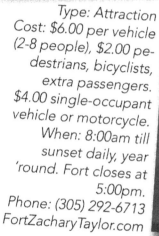

Type: Attraction
Cost: $6.00 per vehicle (2-8 people), $2.00 pedestrians, bicyclists, extra passengers. $4.00 single-occupant vehicle or motorcycle. When: 8:00am till sunset daily, year 'round. Fort closes at 5:00pm.
Phone: (305) 292-6713
FortZacharyTaylor.com

Located at the End of Southard Street, thru Truman Annex

The Ernest Hemingway House and Museum

Ernest Hemingway lived and wrote in Key West for more than ten years. This house was Hemingway's home from 1931 to 1939, although he retained title to the home until he died. Now, it is a private, for-profit landmark and tourist attraction populated by more than forty six-and-seven-toed cats, descendants of Hemingway's first six-toed cat, Snow White, given to him by a ship's captain. Key West is a small island and it is possible that many of the cats on the island are related. The polydactyl cats are not any particular breed. The house stands at an elevation of 16 feet above sea level (the second-highest site on the island). It was originally built in 1851 by Asa Tift, a marine architect and salvage wrecker, in a French Colonial estate style, out of limestone quarried from the site. As testament to its construction and location, it survived many hurricanes, and the deep basement still remains dry. His second wife Pauline found the house for sale at a tax auction in 1931. Her Uncle Gus bought it for her and Ernest for $8,000 cash, and presented it to them as a wedding gift. The house was one of the first on the island to be fitted with indoor plumbing and the first on the island to have an upstairs bathroom with running water, fed from a rain cistern on the roof. Also notable are a built-in fireplace and the first swimming pool in Key West, which was the only pool within 100 miles in the late 30's. Pauline spent $20,000 (equivalent to $330,000 in 2013) to have the deep well-fed pool built for her husband while he was away as a Spanish Civil War correspondent in 1938. When Hemingway returned, he was unpleasantly surprised by the cost and exclaimed, "Well, you might as well have my last cent." This penny is embedded in concrete today near the pool. In 1937, when Ernest was in Spain, Pauline hired Ernest's friend, driver, and handyman, Toby Bruce, to build the high brick wall that surrounds the house today. Hemingway converted a urinal obtained after a renovation at Sloppy Joe's bar into a water fountain in the yard, where it remains a prominent feature at the home, filled with water from a large Cuban jar and serving as one of many water sources for the grounds' cats. His writer's studio in the second floor of a free-standing carriage house, where he stayed briefly in the 1950's when visiting from his home in Cuba, was once connected by a second story walkway to the master bedroom. In 1988, the house was a filming location of the 16th James Bond movie Licence to Kill. In the scene, Bond resigns from the secret service and then flees through the garden. In protection of M, the fictional guards watch from the Key West Lighthouse across the street. Wander freely through the lush grounds. Educated tour guides give insightful narratives and are eager to answer questions. The Hemingway Home Book Store and Gift Shop offers a full array of Ernest Hemingway's novels, poems, short stories and biographies.

Type: Attraction Cost: (Cash only) $14 adult, $6 child, under 5 free, includes a 30-minute guided tour (no reservations needed). When: Year 'round from 9am to 5pm. Phone: (305) 294-1136, weddings (305) 393-2444, bookstore (305) 294-1575, hemingwayhome.com

Located at 907 Whitehead Street

3

Fantasy Fest

Photo by Nick Doll

Fantasy Fest, the mother of all Key West festivals, is an annual 10-day party in paradise for grown-ups that includes fanciful balls, a huge parade, body painting, costume parties and competitions, AIDS fundraisers, a Fantasy Fest King and Queen contest, a Fantasy Fest poster contest, pet and neighborhood parades for the entire family, and lots of alcohol. The highlight of Fantasy Fest is its grand parade featuring humorous floats, including a celebrity Grand Marshall. In recent years, attendance at Fantasy Fest has surpassed 100,000 people, more than three times the population of the island itself. Started in 1979 by a small group of Key West locals, the party was created to bring visitors to the island in what was a typically quiet, but beautiful season. It worked. Fantasy Fest has grown every year since its inception and is now the wildest extravaganza of the year. Fun-loving revelers from around the globe bring their creativity and imaginations as they descend upon Key West each year in October for 10 days filled with costuming, parades, libations, and excitement. Always a theme - such as 'Vampires, Villains and Vixens', 'A-Conch-alypse', and 'Freaks, Geeks and Goddesses'. 2017's theme: "Time Travel Unravels". 2017 events include: the kick-off Goombay Festival (page 23), Royal Coronation Ball, King Neptune's Curse and the Spirits of the Long Dead, Key West Burlesque presents the Sexy Side of Star Wars, the Reddy Ice Fantasy Facade Home and Business Decorating Competition, and the Official Fantasy Fest Poster Signing Party, See the following page for a partial list of the ongoing festival parties. Everyone's invited.

Type: Extreme Party Cost: Free to watch, everything else costs money When: Ten days before the last Saturday of October Contact: 305-295-9112 fantasyfest.com

Photo by Larry Blackburn

(Fantasy Fest, continued)
Here's a partial and constantly evolving list of Fantasy Fest parties you might discover, if you dare: Goombay Festival (page 23), Key West Burlesque (page 95), Super Heroes and Villains 5K Walk and Luau, Tutu Tuesday, Rick's Cocktails for Animal Tails SPCA Animal Party, Plaid Party at Cap'n

Tony's, the Marker's 60's Pool Party, Schooner Wharf's Wharf-stock, Rumor's Luv2Glow Block Dance Party, Dungeon and Dark Secrets Party at 801 Bourbon Bar, the Pet Masquerade and Parade (page 59), Bare Assets Anything but Clothes Party, the Headdress Ball (page 127), Kelly's Kinky Carnival

Caribbean, Lazy Gecko Redneck Party, Dante's Halo and Horns Pool Party, Sloppy Joe's Toga Party, Rick's White Party, Fat Tuesday's Pink Party, Bottlecap's Pajama and Lingerie Party, Señor Frog's Glow Party, Duval Street Fair (on Friday), Lucy's Blue Party, Local's Masquerade March from the KW Cemetery to Duval Street, Sunset Pier Living Art Expo (body painting), Sandbar's Pimp and Ho Party, Bourbon Street Tea Dance Party, Southernmost Costume Contest, Mangoes Dirty Doctors and Naughty Nurses Party, Exposed Clothing-Optional Pool/Hot Tub/Foam Party at the Bourbon Bar, Kinky Couples Party at some discreet downtown location (must apply online), and then the fabulous Fantasy Fest Parade on Saturday night. (Rum Barrel, who hosted the annual Pirate Bash, and Chicago's who hosted the Gangsters and Molls Party both closed this year). On Sunday morning, there is a children's and family day at Bayview Park, and a Fat Lady Sings Tea Dance at LaTeDa. The best way to keep updated is via the official fantasyfest.com web site.

Photo by Nick Doll

2

Type: Experience
Cost: Free, but bring money to tip and shop
When: Year 'round

Mallory Square

Beginning two hours before sunset, 365 days a year, the Sunset Celebration has captivated the imaginations of millions of visitors throughout the decades, including iconic figures like Mark Twain in the 1800s to Tennessee Williams in the late 20th century. People from around the world gather to see magicians, jugglers, clowns, psychics, musicians, artists, and food vendors, that combine for an incredible cultural experience. Don't miss Will Soto's juggling high-wire act, Vaudeviiian Jeep Caillouet and his amazing dog Cleo, Dr. Juice's aerial acrobatics, Dennis Riley the Southernmost Bagpiper, Bible Bill doing his preaching, Dale the sword swallower, Mark Riggs on the 10' suicycle of death, guitarist and songwriter Bert Lee, and many, many more. The one place every Key West visitor should experience, or you really have not been to Key West. And if you're lucky, this is where you'll see the legendary Green Flash. This is real Key West.

Located at the Ends of Whitehead and Front Streets

One Human Family

Key West is the kind of place that inspires diversity, and kindles individuality and acceptance. We have more in common with strangers than we have differences. We all love our families. We all want to be safe. We all want the best for others. We all then must realize a few basic and undeniable facts. Borders are manmade. All races come from some common ancestor. All genders want to achieve to their greatest potential, equally. All religion seeks the same atonement. Age is a state of mind. People are attracted to who they are attracted to, and love who they love. The heart goes where it wants to go. We are all caretakers, of one another, and of all Creation. We are all just individual human beings, all inhabiting this one small blue planet. We all hurt. We all cry. We all dream. We all love. We are one human family. So. Just be you. And love one another.

One family.
Una familia.
एक परिवार.
一家人.
عائلة واحدة.
одна семья.
一つの家族.

SAVE THEM FROM
THEMSELVES...
...VOTE "YES" FOR THE
FENCE AROUND
KEY WEST

YOU ARE
HERE
N 24° 31' 3
W81° 46' 7
THIS IS
PARADISE

ONE HUMAN FAMILY

ALL PEOPLE ARE CREATED EQUAL MEMBERS OF
ONE HUMAN FAMILY

No Shirt, No Shoes
No Problem,
You're in Key West
Everybody's Welcome, C'mon In!

BUSINESS
HOURS:
Mon. 10:30 to 6:00
Tues. 10:30 to 6:00
Wed. 10:30 to 6:00
Thur. 10:30 to 6:00
Fri. 10:

Type: Universal
Cost: Free
When: Always

Photo by Carol Tedesco

Table of Contents (alphabetical)

Thanks to these awesome photographers

Larry Blackburn

Ralph DePalma

Nick Doll

Rob O'Neal

About the photos
A lot of the photos I've used in this book are mine, and my friends'. I've asked permission to use all other photos when I knew (or could find out) who the photographer was, and gave photo credits in each case. I've blatantly used publicity pics from web sites of businesses I've included in this book, and a few stock photos here and there. The problem is that, with the rest, I've been collecting photos from Facebook and the internet and mingling them with my own for years and years, long before I ever dreamed of writing this book, and a lot of them I just don't know or can't remember now, and I have no way of finding out. I'm not trying to screw anybody over here or get away with anything. If you see a photo of yours in this book used without your permission, please notify me. I'll either take it out immediately in the next edition (they're small runs -- this is self-published), or I'll give you a photo credit, or make whatever arrangements are necessary with you to keep it in in future editions. Whatever you would like to do.

Thanks. -- Bucky
buckymontgomery@gmail.com

About the author

Louisville-born Bucky Montgomery is an artist, writer, musician, publisher, host, and a promoter of various annual Key West functions, who has resided in Key West for the better part of twenty years. He writes for the Florida Weekly newspaper, is a regular guest and host on various radio shows, produces the annual Best of Key West singer/songwriter compilation CDs, has seven of his own CDs on iTunes (including two from bands SLAG and Dorothy Boy), is the author of a series of fantasy novels, and has done artwork for businesses all around the world, including Heavy Metal magazine, the San Jose Sharks NHL team, Atari, and the Kentucky Opera. He has bartended, owned a restaurant/bar called Bucky's, worked as a morgue attendant, was a rifleman in an ultralight infantry cohort unit in the United States Army, was a law enforcement officer, and at the opposite end of the spectrum...shhh...he was even a dealer of 'contraband', amongst other careers... His next project is a science thriller called Animal Kingdom - the Extinction Virus, due to drop in Fall 2017. (Added 'Where's Bucky?' bonus: he's featured in 25 photos in this book. Can you find them all, above pic included?)

On the first day of the new millennium, artist JT Thompson started handing out free "One Human Family" stickers to increase awareness that "like fingers on a hand, we appear separate; but each of us are in fact an integral part of each other." He printed 2,000 stickers and biked them every Sunday to shops and businesses around Key West, Florida. They went quickly.

Soon, he had to print more stickers...5,000, 10,000 and then 25,000 at a time as people of all colors, classes, religions, nationalities, orientations and abilities asked for them. On October 17, 2000, the Key West City Commission unanimously adopted "One Human Family" as the city´s official philosophy, declaring "we want to share our unique perspective and simple words of hope ´One Human Family´ with our global neighbors, so others can find inspiration to grow beyond the artificial limitations of racism, nationalism, classism, monotheism, prejudice, homophobia and every other illusion used to try to separate us from all being equal." No city had ever taken such a strong stand to declare the unity and equality of all people, but Key West is not like anywhere else.

JT continued to print stickers and send them out worldwide. In 2001, an all-volunteer non-profit organization was established where 100% of contributions went to printing stickers. In early 2001, the Monroe County Commission unanimously voted ´One Human Family´ as the official philosophy of the county as well.

"One Human Family" has been endorsed by groups as diverse as Carnival Cruise Lines, Tropicana Orange Juice, General Motors´ AFL-CIO and the Simon Weisenthal Holocaust Museum, along with academic groups, clubs and activists across the nation. JT reports that he is now sending out up to 15,000 stickers a month - always for free. Some people even include them when paying bills or in their holiday cards. "The win/win nature of OHF," he explains, "is that people not only get a message of unity and equality, but they also learn that Key West is the most welcoming and inclusive island in the world, which is great for attracting tourism!"

You can obtain free stickers bearing this message from:

One Human Family Educational Foundation
P.O. Box 972, Key West, FL 33041
(A 501(c)3 non-profit, all-volunteer, non-partisan, non-denominational group. 100% of all funds are used to print and distribute more free stickers around the world.)